Captioning and Subtitling for d/Deaf and Hard of Hearing Audiences

Captioning and Subtitling for d/Deaf and Hard of Hearing Audiences

Soledad Zárate

First published in 2021 by
UCL Press
University College London
Gower Street
London WC1E 6BT

Available to download free: www.uclpress.co.uk

ISBN: 978-1-78735-712-9 (Hbk)
ISBN: 978-1-78735-711-2 (Pbk)
ISBN: 978-1-78735-710-5 (PDF)
ISBN: 978-1-78735-713-6 (epub)
ISBN: 978-1-78735-714-3 (mobi)
DOI: https://doi.org/10.14324/111.9781787357105

This book is dedicated to d/Deaf and hard of hearing people.

Contents

List of figures

List of tables

List of abbreviations

ADI	Arts & Disability Ireland
ARD	Arbeitsgemeinschaft der öffentlich-rechtlichen Rundfunkanstalten der Bundesrepublik Deutschland
ASR	automatic speech recognition
AVMSD	Audiovisual Media Services Directive
AVT	audiovisual translation
BAHA	bone-anchored hearing aid
BBC	British Broadcasting Corporation
BCIG	British Cochlear Implant Group
BDA	British Deaf Association
BFI	British Film Institute
BTE	behind-the-ear
BVOD	broadcaster video-on-demand
BW	body-worn
CBBC	Children's British Broadcasting Corporation
CI	cochlear implant
CIC	completely in-the-canal
CRIDE	Consortium for Research into Deaf Education
CRPD	Committee on the Rights of Persons with Disabilities *or* Convention on the Rights of Persons with Disabilities
CRTC	Canadian Radio-television and Telecommunications Commission
dB	decibel
DFXP	Distributed Format Exchange Profile
DSA	Disabled Students' Allowance
DTV	digital television
DVD	digital versatile disc
EAA	European Accessibility Act
EBU	European Broadcasting Union
EFHOH	European Federation of Hard of Hearing People
EUD	European Union of the Deaf

GALMA	Galician Observatory for Media Accessibility
HoH	hard of hearing
HTML	Hypertext Markup Language
ILSA	interlingual live subtitling for access
ITC	International Television Commission *or* in-the-canal
ITE	in-the-ear
ITV	Independent Television
LED	light-emitting diode
LiRICS	Live Reporting International Certification Standard
MAP	Media Accessibility Platform
MHC	model human cochlea
NADP	National Association of Deafened People
NBC	National Broadcasting Company
NCI	National Captioning Institute
NDCS	National Deaf Children's Society
NHS	National Health Service
NHSP	newborn hearing screening programme
ODPS	on-demand programme services
Ofcom	Office of Communications
OHCHR	Office of the (UN) High Commissioner for Human Rights
OTT	over-the-top
PBS	public broadcasting services
RITE	receiver-in-the-ear
SDH	subtitling for d/Deaf and hard of hearing audiences
SFS	speech-following software
SL	sign language
SRT	SubRip text
SSA	SubStation Alpha
STT	speech-to-text transcription
STTR	speech-to-text reporter
TAD	tactile audio display
TDF	Theatre Development Fund
TheatreNI	Theatre Northern Ireland
TTML	Timed Text Markup Language
TVA	Téléviseurs associés
UAB	Universitat Autònoma de Barcelona
UK	United Kingdom
UKCA	UK Cinema Association
UPIAS	Union of the Physically Impaired Against Segregation
USA	United States of America
VOD	video-on-demand

VRM	Vlaamse Regulator voor de Media
VRT	Vlaamse Radio- en Televisieomroep
W3C	World Wide Web Consortium
WebVTT	Web Video Text Tracks
WGBH	Western Great Blue Hill
WHO	World Health Organization
WPM	word per minute
ZDF	Zweites Deutsches Fernsehen
ZHAW	Zürcher Hochschule für Angewandte Wissenschaften/ Zurich University of Applied Sciences

Preface

This book will appeal to anyone with an interest in captioning and subtitling for d/Deaf and hard of hearing people (SDH). Our audiences include people who are deaf or hard of hearing and identify themselves with the mainstream hearing society, as well as members of the linguistic and cultural minority of the Deaf community. It encompasses the experience and knowledge acquired during years of professional work and research in the field.

The book is intended to act as a companion for subtitlers and captioners who may have doubts about how to translate features which are particularly important for this audience, such as music, sound effects and paralanguage. It provides examples from real practice and discusses the thinking processes of a subtitler and captioner.

As a hearing person, I do not feel I can rely on intuition or first-hand personal experience when making subtitling and captioning choices. Understanding the audience is absolutely essential and this is a recurring theme throughout the book and my practice. I wrote a chapter – Chapter 3 – about the audience and its diversity. Even if the one subtitle or caption file will need to cater for all the d/Deaf and hard of hearing people in the audience, understanding the characteristics of the different individuals will give us the necessary perspective to make informed choices. As a matter of course, I always look for opportunities of engagement with my audience so as to be able to deliver work to the highest standard.

I advocate an inclusive approach and embrace the social model of disability. I believe that there is still a great deal that society can do to reduce, and ultimately remove, the disabling barriers encountered by disabled people on a daily basis. Subtitlers and captioners can contribute to the fulfilment of this aim by using their skills to render audiovisual material, live events and performances, as well as theatre plays, inclusive. By captioning the puppet shows at the Puppet Theatre Barge (London), I made the venue inclusive to d/Deaf and hard of hearing audiences, a rewarding experience that taught me that it is indeed possible for individuals to implement a positive change. I firmly believe that legislation is the main step towards changing policies and practices, but it is also empowering to know that it is up to individuals to make this change happen. More about this venture can be read in Chapter 6.

The chapters in the book are self-contained and can be read independently. They have been thought from a pedagogical perspective and include a range of activities for the reader to have a more active role, if desired.

I hope that you enjoy the reading and find some inspiration.

Acknowledgements

I am very grateful to the d/Deaf and hard of hearing people who have given feedback on the captioned performances at the Puppet Theatre Barge since 2016; it has been fundamental to the writing of this book.

I would like to thank the Puppet Theatre Barge for welcoming my initial idea of rendering the venue accessible and for trusting my work.

A very special thanks goes to Professor Jorge Díaz-Cintas for his careful reading of the manuscript and for his many valuable suggestions, which helped me significantly improve and clarify the book.

I am in debt to CEO Melanie Sharpe, captioner Lynn Jackson and the team at Stagetext for engaging with my work and enabling me to meet with them and have insightful conversations with co-founders Merfyn Williams and Peter Pullan. I have learned so much from these two people and their team, and have drawn great inspiration.

Last but not least, I would like to thank Andrew Lambourne for his generosity in agreeing to meet up and answer all my questions about the smart-caption glasses.

1
Subtitling for d/Deaf and hard of hearing audiences

1.1 The history of subtitles

Intertitles, or title cards, are at the origin of subtitles. Intertitles consisted of short sentences, drawn or printed on paper, filmed and placed between sequences of the film. Normally the text was written in white on a black background. They were used mainly to convey dialogue and narrations related to the images (Díaz-Cintas and Remael 2007). They were first seen in 1903 as epic, descriptive titles in Edwin S. Porter's *Uncle Tom's Cabin* (Ivarsson 2004).

In 1927, the first sound film was screened: *The Jazz Singer*. Intertitles disappeared with the end of the silent film era and the new soundtrack had to be replaced by means of subtitles or dubbing. The Netherlands, the Scandinavian countries, Hungary and France were pioneers in developing early subtitling techniques (Ivarsson 2004).

With the advent of sound films, d/Deaf actors lost their jobs. One of them, Emerson Romero, from Cuba, moved to New York in 1947, purchased a number of sound films, inserted intertitles to account for the dialogue exchanges and rented them to Deaf associations. Although this method was successful in giving access to the film to d/Deaf and hard of hearing (HoH) viewers, it was technically unsatisfactory as the film was lengthened considerably (Kovalik 1992).

In 1950, the American Schools for the Deaf found a subtitling solution that consisted in superimposing subtitles upon existing print without having to cut and insert intertitles. The subtitles would appear at the bottom of the screen without interrupting the film (Boatner 1950). An optical subtitling process was developed for television, whereby the subtitles were written on paper and then one-frame stills of each subtitle were shot. The resulting film negative was put in a scanner and fed either manually by the translator or automatically. The writing was generally white on a black background. Where no subtitle was required, blank frames were inserted between subtitle frames (Ivarsson 2004).

The intertitles were not produced with a d/Deaf or hard of hearing audience in mind, but were an adequate tool for this audience to access the film, as any relevant sound-related elements were conveyed in writing. The insertion of intertitles was linked to the pre-production or production stages of the film, whereas the subsequent subtitles for d/Deaf and hard of hearing viewers were, and still generally are, part of the post-production stage. In a way, intertitles were intrinsic to the film, while subtitles for d/Deaf and hard of hearing audiences, being linked to the post-production stage of film-making, are seen as a separate entity. However, researchers such as Romero-Fresco advocate the integration of accessibility as part of the film-making process (Romero-Fresco 2013); Romero-Fresco provides an example of accessible film-making with the film *Joining the Dots* (Romero-Fresco 2012).

In the United Kingdom, the technical evolution of subtitles for d/Deaf and hard of hearing viewers (SDH) culminated in 1979 in the first transmission of a TV programme with subtitles using Ceefax, the world's first Teletext information service, developed by the British Broadcasting Corporation (BBC) in 1971.[1] The programme subtitled was a documentary about d/Deaf children called *Quietly in Switzerland*. During that year, several other programmes were subtitled, including the Queen's Christmas message.

In the 1980s, the first mainland European countries to provide SDH were Flemish-speaking Belgium, France, West Germany, Italy and the Netherlands, followed by Portugal and Spain in the 1990s (Remael 2007).

The United States preceded the United Kingdom and other pioneering European countries by a few years with the provision of SDH – or *captions*, as they are called in American English – for *The French Chef*, aired in 1972 on WGBH, the Public Broadcasting Service (PBS) station licensed to Boston, Massachusetts (Downey 2008). A decade later, in 1982, the National Captioning Institute (NCI) introduced live subtitling, or real-time captioning, to live broadcast events, performed by former court reporters trained as live subtitlers.

Germany was also among the pioneering live subtitling countries, as the broadcaster Arbeitsgemeinschaft der öffentlich-rechtlichen Rundfunkanstalten der Bundesrepublik Deutschland (ARD) introduced subtitled news in 1984 (Remael 2007).

In the United Kingdom, live subtitling using stenography was first launched in 1986 with the programme *Blue Peter* on BBC. A few years later, the Broadcasting Act 1990 came into effect, requiring all public broadcasting stations to 'provide minimum amounts of subtitling for deaf and hard-of-hearing people and to attain such technical standards in the provision of subtitling as the ITC[2] specifies' (UK Parliament 1990, sec. 35). In the 1990s, the modest demand for live subtitling was dealt with by using stenography. As the legislation imposed higher subtitling quotas – the Communications Act 2003 (UK Parliament 2003) demanded that 60 per cent of programmes should be accompanied by subtitles within five years, which was to be increased to 80 to 90 per cent within 10 years – a significant development took place in the 2000s with the introduction of respeaking, a much more financially viable way of subtitling large volumes of live output than the one offered by stenography.

The first live subtitled programme using respeaking in the United Kingdom was the World Snooker Championship, broadcast in April 2001 (Marsh 2006). Simultaneously, similar experiments were being conducted at Vlaamse Radio- en Televisieomroep (VRT), the national Belgian public broadcaster for the Flemish region and at Zweites Deutsches Fernsehen (ZDF), a German public-service television broadcaster. Live subtitling soon expanded rapidly in other European countries, such as Spain, France and Italy, where it was introduced in 2004, 2007 and 2008 respectively (Romero-Fresco 2018). For a detailed discussion of the professional practice of live subtitling, see section 1.4.1.

1.2 SDH within audiovisual translation (AVT)

The term *audiovisual* encompasses programmes that exist through the combination of the visual and auditory channels. Because of the co-existence of these two sensorial channels, audiovisual text has been defined as *polysemiotic* (Gottlieb 1997). Both Delabastita (1989) and Gottlieb (1997) distinguish a total of four communicative dimensions in audiovisual text, using slightly different terminology. Their categories are as follows (Delabastita's / Gottlieb's):

*   visual presentation: verbal signs / verbal visual elements
*   visual presentation: non-verbal signs / non-verbal visual elements
*   acoustic presentation: verbal signs / verbal auditory elements
*   acoustic presentation: non-verbal signs / non-verbal auditory elements.

This categorisation is particularly useful in defining the elements present in programmes subtitled for d/Deaf and hard of hearing viewers. In this type of translation, the acoustic signs or auditory elements are those directly translated, although some visual elements embedded in the film, such as inserts, written communications like letters, and hard subtitles, may also require particular attention because they may interfere with the SDH subtitles. For example, in the case of multilingual films, when a foreign language is spoken, a hard subtitle may appear that translates the dialogue into the main language of the film. The presence of the hard subtitle will need to be taken into account by the SDH subtitler, who may also need to subtitle a non-verbal auditory element, such as a relevant sound effect, for the intended audience. Mouth movements (verbal or non-verbal visual elements, depending on their function, i.e. uttering words or sounds) may be more meaningful in SDH than in the context of subtitling for hearing audiences; and verbal mouth movements are not necessarily linked to lip reading, but may nevertheless act as cues to direct the viewer to the subtitle area of the screen. Gottlieb includes picture composition and flow within the visual non-verbal elements (Gottlieb 1997); to be more specific, gestures, facial expressions and body movements are all part of this category.

As far as auditory elements are concerned, dialogues and lyrics are verbal and are generally translated for hearing viewers watching foreign films, whereas non-verbal auditory elements are peculiar to SDH: they include music, sound effects and paralanguage (i.e. intonation, accent, and information about who is speaking – an identified character, or whether the voice is male or female, for example).

Jakobson (1959) made a distinction between three types of translation that has now become seminal: *intralingual* (or *rewording*), *interlingual* (or *translation proper*) and *intersemiotic* (or *transmutation*, from verbal to non-verbal sign systems). Based on this classification, a distinction has traditionally been made in the field of subtitling between *interlingual subtitling* – that is, the practice that implies translation from one language to another – and *intralingual subtitling* – in which translation takes place within the same language, as in the case of SDH. Because in *intralingual subtitling* there is no translation from a source language into a target language, there were some initial reservations among translation scholars about accepting SDH as falling within the remit of the umbrella term *audiovisual translation* – which traditionally includes such modalities as interlingual subtitling, dubbing and voice-over – but this has now been fully overcome.

SDH is often termed *intralingual subtitling*, reflecting the type of linguistic transfer that characterised subtitles when they first appeared on British television in 1979, followed by other European broadcasters in the 1980s. Nowadays, this definition is reductive, as SDH may also be performed interlingually, particularly on DVDs (Neves 2008) and in streaming. However, instances of SDH on DVDs of foreign films are still quite rare, as there is a tendency to believe that interlingual subtitles for hearing audiences can address the requirements of d/Deaf and hard of hearing viewers (Szarkowska 2013). Similarly, foreign films on video-on-demand platforms are broadcast with interlingual subtitles for hearing viewers. As SDH subtitlers, we know that a translation of only the verbal elements meets the requirements of our audience halfway and it is therefore not completely satisfactory. In traditionally subtitling countries where the progress on accessibility is still limited – such as Greece and Portugal – d/Deaf and hard of hearing viewers may paradoxically have greater, although limited, access to foreign programmes than to programmes produced in their own languages.

In dubbing countries – such as Austria, France, Germany, Italy and Spain – d/Deaf and hard of hearing viewers rely nearly exclusively on the provision of SDH, which is normally performed intralingually from the dubbed version of the programme. This approach somehow confirms that SDH is still placed within an intralingual context rather than being a practice which can also be interlingual. Otherwise, we would have interlingual SDH for programmes with a foreign source language and intralingual SDH for in-house productions. With the development of digitisation and the advent of the DVD in the mid-1990s, viewers around the world – including those in dubbing countries – began to be more exposed to subtitled foreign programmes. Since the turn of the millennium, this experience has become much more common with the arrival of streaming and 'over-the-top' (OTT) distributors, like Amazon Prime Video and Netflix, that provide viewers access to content by sending the media directly through the internet. However, in the majority of cases these subtitles are interlingual, which means that they are not specifically tailored for d/Deaf and hard of hearing audiences.

In addition to the fact that the actual practice is predominantly intralingual, SDH has been associated with intralingual translation because the two main pioneers in the field, the United Kingdom and the United States, are dominated by English-language productions and rarely consume programmes in other languages (Szarkowska 2013).

SDH is one of the various modes within the wider field of AVT that consist of presenting a written text by transcribing the dialogue exchanges, alongside relevant sound effects, music and paralinguistic features for d/Deaf and hard of hearing audiences. In intralingual SDH, discursive elements present in the image, such as signs, letters and inserts, would not require a translation, but in interlingual SDH they would need to be subtitled, as is the case in conventional subtitling for hearing audiences. Besides subtitling verbal information – dialogue lines, lyrics and text present on screen in a foreign language (in interlingual SDH) – relevant non-verbal information is also included, such as intonation, accents (if they are significant) and speaker identification.

1.3 Legislation on accessibility

In terms of regulation at an international level, the Convention on the Rights of Persons with Disabilities (CRPD) is an international human rights treaty issued by the United Nations and aimed at protecting the rights and dignity of people with disabilities. Article 30 of the Convention asserts: 'States Parties recognize the right of persons with disabilities to take part on an equal basis with others in cultural life, and shall take all appropriate measures to ensure that persons with disabilities ... enjoy access to television programmes, films, theatre and other cultural activities, in accessible formats' (United Nations 2006a, Art. 30, para. 1). At the time of writing, 163 countries in the world have signed the Convention (signatories) and 182 have ratified it (States parties) (United Nations 2020a). By signing the treaty, signatories express their agreement with the treaty and their willingness to continue the treaty-making process. Ratifications follow when states give their consent to be legally bound by the treaty.

Article 4 of the Convention urges states to take positive steps to make sure that the human rights of people with disabilities are respected, for example by including the adoption of new laws and policies. In the United Kingdom, the Equality Act (UK Parliament 2010), incorporating the Disability Discrimination Act (UK Parliament 1995) along with other pertinent discrimination legislation, applies. Other examples of national anti-discriminatory legislation are provided by countries such as Australia (Commonwealth Government of Australia 1992), Belgium (Moniteur Belge, 2007) and the United States (United States Congress 1990).

The implementation of the Convention is supported by the Optional Protocol to the Convention on the Rights of Persons with Disabilities (United Nations 2006b), which recognises the competence of the Committee on the Rights of Persons with Disabilities (CRPD), a body of independent experts, to monitor the implementation of the Convention by the States parties. In practical terms, all States parties are obliged to submit regular reports to the Committee on how the rights are being respected, initially within two years of ratification of the Convention and thereafter every four years. The Committee, on the basis of the reports, may make suggestions to the States parties and may also examine individual complaints with regard to alleged violations of the Convention by States parties. To this date, 94 countries in the world have signed the Optional Protocol and 97 have ratified it (United Nations 2020b).

Access to the physical environment, to transportation, and to information and communication (including technologies and systems), is one of the eight principles set out by the Convention in Article 3 and regulated in Article 9 (United Nations 2006a). States parties are required to adopt appropriate standards and guidelines for the provision of information in accessible formats. The Convention (United Nations 2006a) and the Protocol (United Nations 2006b) can be considered a first step towards the regulation of accessibility at an international level. Since its inception in 2006, 181 States and the EU have ratified the Convention, representing 94 per cent of all the member states of the United Nations (2020a).

At a European level, and in consonance with the recommendation of the Commission of the European Communities stating that 'Member States should take all the measures necessary to ensure that all terrestrial television broadcasting services use digital transmission technology and cease using analogue transmission technology on their territory by 1 January 2012' (European Union 2009, 3), all member states have completed the switch-over from analogue to digital television (DTV), as shown in Table 1.1.

Digital technology opened up new possibilities for research, practice and broadcasting as a myriad of solutions previously non-existent in an

Table 1.1   Completion of digital switch-over by member states of the EU

Member state(s)	Date of switch-over
Luxembourg	2006
Finland, Sweden	2007
Denmark	2009
Belgium, Croatia, Estonia, Latvia, Spain	2010
Austria, Cyprus, France, Malta, Netherlands, Slovenia	2011
Czech Republic, Ireland, Germany, Italy, Lithuania, Portugal, Slovakia	2012
Bulgaria, Hungary, Poland	2013
Greece	2014
Romania	2018

Source: ITU 2020

analogue context became available. To mention some of the advantages, digital television allows greater flexibility, higher-resolution pictures, better sound quality, the use of a wider range of colours and a multitude of complex fonts. However, in practice, the potential of digital technology does not seem to be fully exploited when it comes to the layout of the text, and the changes in the presentation of digital subtitles, if any, are rather minimal when these subtitles are compared with the teletext subtitles of the analogue period. For programmes broadcast and subtitled before the advent of digital television, the old subtitle files produced for transmission in analogue television, using teletext, are still commonly used, most likely for financial reasons. Some of the guidelines, such as the ones produced by the BBC (2009), have been revisited, but the main changes present in the current ones (BBC 2019) are attributable to the inclusion of information related to online subtitle work.

The current European legislation is covered by the Audiovisual Media Services Directive (AVMSD), which states:

> The right of persons with a disability and of the elderly to participate and be integrated in the social and cultural life of the Union is inextricably linked to the provision of accessible audiovisual media services. The means to achieve accessibility should include, but need not be limited to, sign language, subtitling, audio-description and easily understandable menu navigation. (European Union 2010, para. 46)

In 2016, the European Commission published a proposal (European Commission 2016) to amend the AVMSD to bring it into line with the rapidly changing audiovisual media landscape and specifically the increase of access to video-on-demand content. This proposal was criticised by the European Union of the Deaf (EUD) as it excluded Article 7, present in the original AVMSD, which stated: 'Member States shall encourage media service providers under their jurisdiction to ensure that their services are gradually made accessible to people with a visual or hearing disability' (European Union 2010, chap. 3). The decision to make this exclusion was justified by the inception of the European Accessibility Act (EAA), a proposal that was designed to create such accessibility obligations for television and that became law in 2019 (European Union 2019). EUD argued that the AVMSD and the EAA should complement each other, in that compulsory accessibility targets should be set in the AVMSD and functional requirements included in the EAA. As a result of these negotiations, the current, amended AVMSD includes Article 7, which is more than an encouragement and explicitly states: 'Member States shall ensure, without undue delay, that services provided by media service providers under their jurisdiction are made continuously and progressively more accessible to persons with disabilities through proportionate measures' (European Union 2018, sec. 11).

The passing of legislation on media accessibility – together with the practice of lobbying, an increase in research experiments and publications, and the manufacture of new technical solutions – has led to rapid developments in this field. Paradoxically, though, information about them is not always easily accessible, as it is scattered across different repositories and languages around the world. The Media Accessibility Platform (MAP) (https://mapaccess.uab.cat/accessometer) is an initiative that tries to remedy this situation by providing a unified atlas of the worldwide landscape of media accessibility, which covers various aspects of this field, including research, national policies, training and professional practices.

1.3.1 Television and video-on-demand quotas

International regulations alongside the practice of lobbying, which plays a significant role in the United Kingdom, has resulted in the adoption of legislation at a national level. The Office of Communications (Ofcom) (https://www.ofcom.org.uk) acts as the independent regulator of the UK communications industries, and one of its many obligations is the promotion of television access services, namely subtitling, signing and audio description. The main role of Ofcom in this area, from its inception in 2003 until the present day, has been to set out the targets for television access services, that is, the obligations, in terms of percentage of services, that each broadcaster has to meet on television and, more recently, in video-on-demand services. Ofcom requires that the BBC channels subtitle 100 per cent of their programme content (Ofcom 2017). The target for ITV1 and Channel 4 is 90 per cent, and for Channel 5 it is 80 per cent (Ofcom 2017). Following the campaign *Subtitle it!*, launched by the British association Action on Hearing Loss (https://www.actiononhearingloss.org.uk) in 2015, the legislation has been extended to video-on-demand services, as contemplated in the Digital Economy Act (UK Parliament 2017). Ofcom has made recommendations to the Government on regulations to improve the accessibility of on-demand programme services (ODPS) (Ofcom 2018) and is currently supporting the Government's drafting of regulations. iPlayer, the online streaming and catch-up service of the BBC, will be at an advantage as back in 2015 it was already providing voluntarily subtitling for 98 per cent of all of its available programming (EFHOH 2015).

Countries that are pioneering in accessibility tend to have solid legislation in place on subtitling provision on television, but less so on video-on-demand (VOD) content, which is a very recent trend in media consumption. The exceptions are the United States and Canada, where subtitling provision of VOD content is regulated.

In the USA, the Federal Communications Commission regulates the industry, requiring that 100 per cent of new programming and 75 per cent of pre-rule (i.e. analogue video programming broadcast before 1998) programming is subtitled (GPO 2019).[3] Video clips that have been broadcast on television with subtitles must also be subtitled when shown on the internet.

In Canada, the obligation to subtitle 100 per cent of content broadcast between 6 am and midnight has been statutory since 2007 (CRTC 2007). This requirement was subsequently extended to advertising and to subtitled television content made available online (CRTC 2015).

In France, public national TV channels – such as Arte, France 2, France 3, France 5, M6, W9 – and private channels – such as Canal+, C8, TF1, TMC – subtitle 100 per cent of their content, as required by law (CSA 2018).

In the Flemish region of Belgium, the Media Decree of 27 March 2009 (VRM 2009) on radio and television broadcasting set subtitling quotas as high as 90 per cent for news and current affairs broadcast content on public and private television. A more recent decree (VRM 2012) increased the target to 100 per cent for news programmes, while a significant, but unquantified, proportion of other genres is expected to be subtitled. Data shows that 100 per cent of content broadcast on public television is subtitled and private channels are not far from reaching the same target (EFHOH 2015).

Public television in Sweden also reaches 100 per cent subtitle provision, whereas private channels are approaching 70 per cent (EFHOH 2015). It is clear that legislation is an important first step towards accessibility. Since 2017, broadcasting companies in Sweden have had to submit yearly reports to the Swedish Press and Broadcasting Authority specifying how they have promoted the accessibility of their channels (Swedish Press and Broadcasting Authority 2016). Specific obligations were imposed on TV4 AB, the largest commercial television channel in Sweden, which was expected to reach 100 per cent of broadcasting time in 2016 for pre-recorded programmes and 55 per cent of broadcasting time for live broadcasts (Swedish Press and Broadcasting Authority 2016).

The statutory subtitling requirement in the Netherlands, traditionally one of the leading countries in the field of SDH, is 95 per cent of national Dutch-language public television and 50 per cent of private television programmes, as regulated respectively by Articles 15 and 17 of the Mediabesluit ('media decree') 2008 (Raad van State 2008). The provision of subtitles is approaching 100 per cent on public television and 65 per cent on private channels (EFHOH 2015). The lack of legislation on VOD content has not stopped Uitzending Gemist, the Dutch national online catch-up provider, from delivering subtitling on 97 per cent of its online broadcasts (EFHOH 2015).

While Belgium (Flanders), Canada, France, the Netherlands, Sweden and the USA are pioneering in terms of legislation and subtitle provision, other countries, such as Austria, the Czech Republic, Denmark, Finland, Slovenia and Spain are making good progress (EFHOH 2015).

1.3.2 SDH at the cinema

In the case of cinema exhibition in the United Kingdom, all releases from large distributors (e.g. Universal, Warner Bros.) and most releases from medium-sized distributors include subtitles for d/Deaf and hard of hearing viewers ('captions' in American English), whereas the provision of SDH by independent distributors relies on the budget. The UK film release schedule by the Film Distributors' Association (https://filmdistributorsassociation.com/release-schedule/past-present-and-future-releases/) includes details of subtitled releases. It is clear that, at least for mainstream cinema releases, the subtitles are made available by the distributors, but in practice most screenings are not inclusive. This is likely to be the result of a lack of legislation in this area. The exception is the USA, where the legislation in place requires that cinemas have and maintain the equipment necessary to provide SDH at a film patron's seat when showing a digital movie which is made available with subtitles (Department of Justice, Civil Rights Division 2016).

In the United Kingdom, the provision of SDH at the cinema is not regulated at present. That said, the United Kingdom and Sweden are the two countries in Europe in which subtitling in the cinema is becoming increasingly frequent for the newest releases (EFHOH 2015). Subtitles in UK cinemas are currently *open*, that is, visible to all viewers in the audience, and this is perhaps the main reason why not all subtitled releases are screened with subtitles. The subtitle and video files are synchronised through an electronic subtitling system, with which most, if not all, mainstream cinemas are equipped. Most cinemas have digital subtitle built-in facilities; for 35mm film systems, the transmission of subtitles requires the installation of either the DTS-CSS Cinema Subtitling System or Dolby ScreenTalk, where the subtitles are superimposed over the projected image, without the need of overlaying them onto the film itself.

There have been attempts in the past to offer targeted solutions to d/Deaf and hard of hearing viewers, which are made available on an individual basis. The subtitle glasses developed by Sony constitute an example; the subtitles are displayed onto the screen of the glasses and become superimposed on the cinema screen, with the advantage of not requiring viewers to refocus, as they have to when using small seat-mounted displays (BBC 2011). Subtitle glasses are widely available in the United States but, up till now, this solution does not seem to have become popular in other parts of the world and there is no readily available evidence of cinemas having adopted it in the United Kingdom.

Another, more recent, solution in this direction is the Off-Screen Cinema Subtitle System (Disabled World 2016), which uses a special display below the main film screen, where the subtitles become visible only to those wearing the special glasses, and is seen as a dark grey area by the other patrons. The system was tested in Cineworld Milton Keynes on 7 February 2014 and, since then, has found support in the form of feedback, testing and promotion from the Regal Entertainment Group in the USA and Regal Cinemas in the UK, the UK Cinema Association and the cinema chain Odeon. Inventor Jack Ezra, of 3D Experience UK (https://www.3dexperience.co.uk), attempted to raise the necessary funds for the prototype to be made available in cinemas worldwide, but his initiative was unsuccessful.

Legislation is a clear step towards accessibility, and lobbying plays a very important role in initiating changes in the United Kingdom and elsewhere. An exemplary initiative in this respect is the *Subtitle it!* campaign for video-on-demand content spearheaded by Action on Hearing Loss, which led to the extension of the existing legislation on material available for broadcast to VOD content. Similarly, there have been petitions, to the UK Cinema Association (UKCA: a body representing the interests of over 90 per cent of UK cinema stakeholders) and to both mainstream and independent cinemas, aimed at increasing the number of subtitled screenings and at having them screened at more varied times of the day (https://www.change.org/p/uk-cinema-association-cinemas-to-show-more-subtitled-films-at-reasonable-times; https://www.change.org/p/petition-uk-multiplex-cinemas-to-dedicate-one-screen-to-subtitled-screenings-for-deaf-people). The petitions refer to open subtitles, but in 2018 the UK Cinema Association, in partnership with Action on Hearing Loss, launched the Technology Challenge Fund, which was intended to stimulate innovations in the delivery of closed-caption subtitling systems for d/Deaf and hard of hearing people. Interestingly, the solution was not to interfere with the experience of hearing viewers, but to allow patrons 'to view subtitles without disturbing other viewers who do not want to view subtitles' (UKCA 2018). The London Short Film Festival hosted the first UK pilot in cinemas of the National Theatre's smart-caption glasses at the British Film Institute (BFI) in January 2020, where four screenings were made available to be experienced with the glasses. For more details about the introduction of the smart-caption glasses at the National Theatre, see section 6.1.2. Arguably, it is not a matter just of changing or updating legislation, but also of raising public awareness of the reasons why d/Deaf and hard of hearing viewers need subtitles so that they can enjoy equal rights with hearing people, as established by the Convention on the Rights of Persons with Disabilities (CRPD) (United Nations, 2006a).

1.4 The SDH subtitler

Once it is established that SDH falls within the remit of the umbrella term audiovisual translation, it becomes clear that the position of the subtitler responsible for SDH is different from that of the subtitler for the hearing audience. The SDH subtitler, similarly to the subtitler for the hearing audience, translates verbal information (dialogue exchanges, narration, etc.). However, while the latter always translates interlingually, the SDH subtitler translates mainly, but not only, intralingually. The SDH subtitler, unlike the subtitler for hearing audiences, also has to translate sounds that are non-verbal and peculiar to SDH, namely music, sound effects, intonation, accents and voices (i.e. who is speaking).

Besides possessing a broad knowledge of the foreign language, interlingual subtitlers need to have good translation skills and an understanding of film language. Linguistic proficiency and technical dexterity are also part of the subtitlers' toolkit. Although training is key in developing these skills, some decisions may ultimately rely on intuition and experience. The SDH subtitler, in the great majority of cases, will be a hearing individual and therefore less inclined to make intuitive judgements that are based on personal experience. In an ideal scenario, SDH should be performed by a team of hearing and d/Deaf or hard of hearing subtitlers, though this happens very rarely for obvious financial reasons. As a result, in the training of SDH subtitlers, the programme of study needs to include and address, in addition to the traditional subtitling skills, the sociolinguistic requirements of a target audience that has limited or no access to the auditory channel.

The freelance SDH subtitler working on pre-recorded programmes for broadcast, or on films to be exhibited at the cinema, streamed on online platforms or published on DVDs/Blu-rays, may on occasions be working with a transcript of the dialogues. In the case of intralingual SDH, the dialogue exchanges may require some editing, as recommended by some subtitling style guidelines, although the main challenges will probably revolve around decisions about when to insert specific SDH elements, such as sound effects, music, paralinguistic features and the like (see Chapter 5, 'Specific requirements'). In the globalised world we live in, it is very common for clients to require the translation of one audiovisual programme into multiple languages. An English template, that is, a list of subtitles with their in and out times, may be used as a masterfile to make the process more economical and financially viable. On occasions, the subtitles used in the English template end up being used as SDH subtitles, a practice to be discouraged as it fails to include relevant non-verbal sounds and information that is of paramount importance for the d/Deaf and hard of hearing audience.

When SDH was formally introduced in the broadcast industry, in the 1980s, the professional figure of the SDH subtitler did not exist. In the early years, this task was normally performed by multimedia technicians working in broadcasting and consisted mainly of a transcription of the dialogue, the identification of speakers and the representation of sound effects. Music and paralinguistic features, such as accents, pronunciation and intonation, were very rarely conveyed. Some years later, broadcasters, such as the BBC, developed their own set of guidelines and subtitlers started being trained in-house. Formal training in university programmes only commenced in the early 2000s. These days, many universities around the world offer modules on SDH as part of their programmes in translation, at both undergraduate and postgraduate levels: Antwerp, Autònoma de Barcelona, Brasilia, City, University of London, Dijon, Fortaleza, Granada, Jaume I (Castellón), Leeds, Lille, Macerata, Roehampton, Salvador de Bahia, Sevilla, Stockholm, Surrey, Turin, and University College London are examples of institutions that have embraced the teaching of this professional practice. Subtitlers with academic training in SDH are at an advantage when entering the industry, but many SDH subtitlers have a subtitling background with no accessibility training or even a translation background. In the latter case, the required training may be completed in-house or by attendance at a professional course in SDH, like the ones offered by Roehampton and University College London, which can be either face-to-face or online.

SDH subtitlers working for OTT corporations like Netflix may be using the company's own cloud-based subtitling suite; Originator is the one used by Netflix. However, to a freelance subtitler working for several clients, investing in specialist subtitling software often becomes a necessity. Available options in an exclusively Windows environment include EZTitles (https://www.eztitles.com), Lemony Subtitler (http://www.lemonysubtitler.com), and Wincaps Q4 (https://broadstream.com/products/wincaps). Spot Software (https://www.spotsoftware.nl) is among the very few specialist subtitling software programs compatible with MacOS as well as Windows, whereas Annotation Edit (http://www.zeitanker.com/content/tools/zeitanker_tools/zeitanker_annotation_edit) is only compatible with MacOS. Most programs are available with a free trial and can be either rented or purchased. Cloud-based platforms specifically designed for subtitling include CaptionHub (https://www.captionhub.com) and OOONA (https://ooona.net), both offering demo versions. Students and subtitlers at the beginning of their careers may benefit from experimenting with the several freeware alternatives, which are also used by some professional subtitlers, working in both Mac and Windows environments: Aegisub (http://www.aegisub.org), Amara (https://amara.org), Belle Nuit (https://www.belle-nuit.com/belle-nuit-subtitler), Subtitle Edit (https://www.nikse.dk/subtitleedit), and Subtitle Workshop (http://subworkshop.sourceforge.net). Subs Factory (https://www.subsfactory.app) is compatible with Macs only, whereas VisualSubSync (https://www.videohelp.com/software/VisualSubSync) is Windows-based.

1.4.1 The live subtitler

The profile of the SDH subtitler, particularly for in-house positions, has changed with the advent of live subtitling for broadcasts, live events and conferences. The subtitler may be combining work for pre-recorded programmes with live subtitling; the latter, in most cases, will require training in respeaking, defined by Romero-Fresco as:

a technique in which a respeaker listens to the original sound of a (live) programme or event and respeaks it, including punctuation marks and some specific features for the deaf and hard-of-hearing audience, to a speech recognition software, which turns the recognized utterances into subtitles displayed on the screen with the shortest possible delay. (Romero-Fresco 2011, 1)

Although the aim is to subtitle verbatim, high speech rates, combined with the need to dictate punctuation marks, mean that the respeaker ends up paraphrasing rather than repeating the original soundtrack to speech recognition software, such as Dragon's Naturally Speaking.

All the in-house subtitling opportunities available in the United Kingdom in companies such as Red Bee Media include respeaking in the job description. Since 2007 respeaking has been introduced in universities – such as Universitat Autònoma de Barcelona (UAB), the University of Antwerp, the University of Leeds, the University of Roehampton, the University of Vigo and Zurich University of Applied Sciences (ZHAW) – as part of their translation curriculum. Universities respond to the demands of the industry, and the live subtitler, who may combine the knowledge acquired at university with in-house training provided by the company, is a highly qualified figure.

As described in section 1.1, live subtitling was originally performed using speech-to-text transcription (STT), that is, transcription of the verbal elements executed by a stenographer with a shorthand keyboard. The sounds are typed phonetically and then converted into English text by specific software. The advantage of this type of live subtitling is that the stenographer is able to keep up with the speed of speech.

This technique, developed in the 1970s as an initiative of the BBC's Ceefax teletext service, was abandoned in the United Kingdom and superseded by respeaking in the 2000s. The inception of respeaking dates back to the early 1940s; it originated in the United States for court reporting. Respeaking is also the preferred method for live subtitling in countries like Belgium, France, Spain and Switzerland. In the United States, since its introduction in 1982, broadcasters to this day have relied on speech-to-text reporters or stenographers to deliver the subtitles. In Canada and Italy, steno-made live subtitles for television are also more common than respoken subtitles (Romero-Fresco 2018). Interestingly, live subtitling in the past, and before the advent of respeaking, was also performed by subtitlers using a conventional alphanumeric keyboard at a fast typing speed.

The reason companies such as the BBC and VRT, having worked with broadcast stenography in the past, turned to respeaking later on is the training required, which is much less strenuous for respeakers than that required to become a speech-to-text reporter (STTR) or a stenographer, besides being less costly. Although the output of the subtitles achieved using stenotype keyboards can be verbatim – skilled stenographers type up to 300 words per minute – and the level of accuracy is much greater, the quality of the subtitles relies on the shorthand skills of the speech-to-text reporter and the training can take between two and five years.

Academic training in respeaking is very limited and is often offered as part of larger modules on subtitling for d/Deaf and hard of hearing audiences (Romero-Fresco 2012), for example at the University of Leeds in the United Kingdom. More in-depth options are offered by the University of Roehampton in the United Kingdom, the Universitat Autònoma de Barcelona and the Universidade de Vigo in Spain, and the University of Antwerp in Belgium. Training takes between one and six months and is almost exclusively intralingual, with the exception of the University of Antwerp, where an English-to-Dutch component is offered (Romero-Fresco 2018). Interlingual respeaking training is likely to be introduced in more universities in the future to meet the increasing demand for interlingual live subtitlers from broadcasters as well as political and educational institutions. As a response to the demands of the industry, the Interlingual Live Subtitling for Access (ILSA) project (http://galma observatory.webs.uvigo.es/projects/interlingual-live-subtitling-for-access-ilsa) came about in 2017 with the aim of developing a framework for this rather new professional figure and to implement interlingual live subtitles on television, in the classroom, and in social and political settings.

Another recent development in the field is LiRICS (Live Reporting International Certification Standard) (http://galmaobservatory.webs.uvigo.es/services/certification), the first worldwide certification process for professional respeakers, set up by the Galician Observatory for Media Accessibility (GALMA) as a response to the United Kingdom government's refusal, in 2016, to use the Disabled Students' Allowance (DSA) to provide respoken subtitles to students, on the basis that respeaking was not a qualified profession (Romero-Fresco et al. 2019). Since the Department of Education in the United Kingdom agreed in 2019 that LiRICS meets their requirements, d/Deaf and hard of hearing students can now use their Disabled Students' Allowance to engage a respeaker. In the long term, this certification may also have an impact on the wider recognition of respeaking as a profession.

Although this will certainly change in the future, as respeaking is gradually introduced into academia, at present many companies deliver this training in-house. A recent survey was conducted among

126 respeakers from 27 countries across the world, including Australia, Austria, Belgium, Brazil, Canada, China, Germany, India, Iran, Korea, Malaysia, the Netherlands, New Zealand, Poland, South Africa, Spain, Switzerland and the United Kingdom. The majority of respondents, 96, were intralingual live subtitlers, nine respondents were working on interlingual live subtitling, and 21 worked as both intralingual and interlingual respeakers (Robert, Schrijver and Diels 2019).

Among the group of intralingual respeakers, a substantial majority, 76 per cent (N=71), had been trained exclusively in-house, while only 6 per cent (N=6) had been academically trained. The remaining group had received vocational or combined training. Among the interlingual respeakers, 45 per cent (N=10) had been trained in-house, while 41 per cent (N=9) had been academically trained. Again, the remaining group had received vocational or combined training. In-house training can take up to three months. Among 72 of respondents who trained in-house, 48 per cent underwent training that lasted between one week and three months, while 39 per cent trained on the job and 13 per cent had up to four days of training (Robert, Schrijver and Diels 2019).

In practice, trained respeakers repeat everything they hear in the programme audio into an automatic speech recognition (ASR) engine, typically Dragon's Naturally Speaking. The engine is trained to their voice and feeds the live subtitling platform – Subito in the case of Red Bee Media – where there is an opportunity to correct the output as it comes out in real time. The accuracy of the live subtitles is dependent on the acoustic conditions, the spoken punctuation and the delivery of speech. For the voice recognition software to recognise the respeaker's voice, the delivery has to be rather unnatural compared to the way we normally speak; every word needs to be spoken clearly, every syllable needs to be stressed and words need to be spaced out. Punctuation is dictated to the software and there are some differences among countries: for example, punctuation at the Téléviseurs associés (TVA) network in Canada is added using a joystick (Romero-Fresco 2018). The respeaker is also responsible for identifying speakers, by initially labelling different speakers with different colours – white, yellow, cyan and green in the United Kingdom – and then selecting the appropriate colour from a keyboard before respeaking each speech. A further responsibility is to reposition the subtitle on screen, if required, so that important action on screen is not obscured by the subtitle. As the task is rather stressful, respeakers are on air for a maximum of 15 minutes at a time with breaks of 15 minutes in between.

We are all familiar with subtitle errors that these days go immediately onto social media. A memorable mistake occurred during the BBC's coverage of the Chinese New Year in 2014. 'Welcome to the year of the whores. People around the world celebrate', read the subtitle, when of course *horse* was intended. In a profession where synchronisation between spoken utterances and written subtitles is of the essence, there is an interplay between delay and accuracy in live subtitling. Corrections made before the subtitle is launched (cued) cause greater delay ('latency') but favour accuracy. In the United Kingdom, to reduce the delay, live subtitles are only corrected after the error appears on the viewers' screens and the correction is introduced by a double hyphen (--). In Belgium, Spain and Switzerland, respeakers make corrections before cueing the subtitles, which creates more delay. In France, accuracy is favoured over timing; three professionals are involved in the process: a respeaker, a corrector – who corrects mistakes – and a whisperer – who suggests corrections to the corrector (Romero-Fresco 2018).

The figure of the subtitler has evolved substantially in the last decades, as the technology has improved, the professional practice has changed and the demand for live subtitlers has increased. What will happen in the future? In Japan, live subtitlers edit and cue live subtitles that have been automatically recognised, while in Portugal some broadcasters use automatic speech recognition systems without any human intervention (Romero-Fresco 2018).

1.5 Discussion points

1.5.1   Watch *Uncle Tom's Cabin* (https://www.youtube.com/watch?v=2zPzz9m0huc). Identify similarities and differences between intertitles and subtitles.

1.5.2   Find a silent film from your country and compare the intertitles to the ones in *Uncle Tom's Cabin*.

1.5.3   Watch the preview of *The Jazz Singer* (https://www.youtube.com/watch?v=4gu7zgWxNRc) and compare it with *Uncle Tom's Cabin*. In which way is *The Jazz Singer* similar to a silent film? How is it different from a modern film?

1.5.4   Find out when subtitles were first broadcast on television in your country. Were they aimed at d/Deaf and hard of hearing viewers?

1.5.5   Can you find any examples of interlingual SDH in your country?

1.5.6   Is SDH regulated in your country? Who sets the targets for broadcasters, and what are they?

1.5.7 To what extent is SDH used in cinemas in your country? Are there any groups attempting to change the practice?

1.5.8 Watch the live streaming of NBC news (https://www.nbcnews.com/now) and BBC news (https://www.bbc.co.uk/news/av/10318089/bbc-news-channel), or the equivalent in your country, and compare the subtitles.

1.5.9 Watch *Captioning – Behind the Scenes* (https://www.youtube.com/watch?v=pqOi4hhlFAU) and identify the main differences and skills required for live subtitling between using respeaking and using stenography.

Notes

1   Ceefax was launched in 1974, as was Oracle, another teletext service, for use by Channel 4 and ITV. In 1993 Teletext replaced Oracle on Channel 4 and ITV, and in 2002 the service was introduced to Channel 5. Teletext was withdrawn from Channel 4, Channel 5 and ITV in 2009, while Ceefax continued to exist until 2012, when the switch-over from analogue to digital television took place.

2   The Independent Television Commission (ITC), established by the Broadcasting Act 1990, was responsible for licensing and regulating commercial television services in the United Kingdom between 1991 and 2003, when it was superseded by the Office of Communications (Ofcom).

3   There are two categories of exemptions. If complying with the subtitling rules is 'economically burdensome', an exemption may be granted upon request. The same applies to 'self-implementing' programmes, which include public service announcements shorter than 10 minutes and not paid for with federal dollars, programming shown from 2 am to 6 am, and programming that is primarily textual.

2
Who is our audience?

2.1 Models of deafness and disabilities

It is important to bear in mind that d/Deaf, deafened and hard-of-hearing people constitute a very diverse group, which includes the Deaf community, whose members consider themselves to be part of a linguistic and cultural minority, but also people who may identify themselves with mainstream hearing society. The term *Deaf* with a capital *D* refers to the group of people who have a strong Deaf identity and disassociate themselves from those who identify linguistically and culturally with mainstream society. *Deafened* usually refers to a person who becomes deaf as an adult. In the United Kingdom, the National Association of Deafened People (NADP) (https://www.nadp.org.uk), founded in 1984, represents primarily deafened people, but also other deaf people who have a spoken language as their main language.

People belonging to the Deaf community do not consider deafness to be a disability and embrace the values upheld by the *cultural model of Deafness*. 'Why should anyone expect deaf people to deny their roots when every other cultural group proudly celebrates its traditions and history? Why stigmatize the speakers of a particular language as disabled?' enquire those belonging to the Deaf community (Dolnick 1993, 41). Cochlear implantation is denounced by some, while other technological advances, such as subtitling, are welcome as they do not alter the Deaf person but adjust the environment to their requirements (Dolnick 1993).

This leads us to the distinction between the medical and social models of disability. The traditional *medical model of disability* is the normative model that identifies the individual medical condition as the disability that needs to be fixed or cured, whereas the *social model of disability* considers the attitudes and structures of society to be the cause of the disability (Oliver 2013; Finkelstein 1980). In other words, disability is seen as a social construct whereby the individual is disabled by the obstacles posed by society.

The *social model of disability* is embedded in the Preamble of the Convention on the Rights of Persons with Disabilities (CRPD), which recognises 'that disability is an evolving concept and that disability results from the interaction between persons with impairments and attitudinal and environmental barriers that hinders their full and effective participation in society on an equal basis with others' (United Nations 2006a, Preamble, para. 5). While the impairment may be physical or mental and resides in the individual, the disablement or disability is imposed by society, through physical and sensory barriers or discriminatory attitudes.

The concept of disability being a social construct may be embraced by members of the Deaf community, but some of the notions advocated by the *social model of disability* – namely the view of deafness as an impairment or the focus on creating all-inclusive environments – are not shared. Members of the Deaf community would consider themselves as happily diverse and different rather than impaired or disabled and would choose to send their children to school for the Deaf rather than mainstream schools.

The principles of the *social model of disability* were formulated in the 1970s by the Union of the Physically Impaired Against Segregation (UPIAS), a disability rights organisation based in the United Kingdom. The organisation's manifesto stated: 'What we are interested in, are ways of changing our conditions of life, and thus overcoming the disabilities which are imposed on top [sic] our physical impairments by the way this society is organised to exclude us' (Union of the Physically Impaired Against Segregation 1974). Rather than being a theoretical concept, the *social model of disability* was meant to change the way society viewed disability (Oliver 1990).

Despite the acknowledgement of deaf people's rights in policy statements, the thinking that characterises the medical model of disability and deafness is, more often than not, based on practice and intervention. A couple of examples that illustrate this point of view are the increase observed in recent decades in the number of children who are given a cochlear implant and the steady decrease in the age of implantation (Brennan 2003).

The provision of captions in a theatre or SDH at the cinema is supportive of an inclusive model. By providing accessible content, we are removing those existing barriers that prevent our audience from having the same access to entertainment as a hearing audience. It is a matter of respect for the differences and of equality.

In the field of SDH, while addressing some misconceptions that surround the discipline, Neves argues that attempts should be made to produce *inclusive* rather than *accessible* audiovisual media (Neves 2008). In other words, audiovisual experiences should be implemented in such a way as to include as many people as possible. The existence of deafness may lead to a different experience of the audiovisual product on the part of the viewer. In this sense, the experience may be more visual than auditory, without implying any lack or disadvantage, especially if the requirements of the audience in question are known and being taken account of through the implementation of the appropriate accessible services.

2.2 A spoken language for d/Deaf and hard-of-hearing audiences

The diversity of the group of d/Deaf and hard-of-hearing people is better reflected in their preferred method(s) of communication, which may include spoken language, sign language or both.

Deafness is measured by determining the loudness of the quietest sound heard, using decibels (dB). People who are not affected by deafness can hear sounds at 20 dB or less across all frequencies. Over 5 per cent (466 million) of the entire population worldwide (7.6 billion) – or one person out of 20 – is affected by *disabling* deafness, that is, a degree greater than 40 dB in the better-hearing ear in adults and a degree greater than 30dB in the better-hearing ear in children (WHO 2020). The majority of people with disabling deafness live in low- and middle-income countries (WHO 2020). Fifteen per cent of the world's adult population is affected by some degree of deafness (WHO 2013). This last percentage matches the national statistics for the United Kingdom, where 11 million of the entire population (66 million) are affected by deafness – that is, one in six or 16 per cent (Hearing Link 2018).

Nearly 0.8 per cent (or 84,000, out of a total of 151,000 signers) of the d/Deaf population in the United Kingdom have sign language as their preferred method of communication (BDA 2020). These people belong to the Deaf community and may have English as a second or third language. The statistics are interesting for subtitlers and captioners who wish to gain knowledge about the preferred method of communication of their audiences. The same data suggests that the majority of d/Deaf people in the United Kingdom have a spoken language as their main method of communication.

Knowing to what extent the d/Deaf and hard-of-hearing audience has had auditory exposure to the spoken language before acquiring deafness can be of guidance to the subtitler or captioner when they make decisions on how to convey elements such as music and sound effects. New SDH subtitlers often wonder whether information about the artist, the title of a song or the instruments being played is meaningful to d/Deaf and hard-of-hearing people. Although this will depend on the specific clip and other factors – such as genre and relevance – subtitlers should not assume a lack of knowledge or experience of the (acoustic) world on the part of their audiences.

As previously mentioned, taking the entire population of the United Kingdom, one in six people, or 16 per cent, are affected by deafness. One to two babies in 1,000 newborns, which is 0.15 per cent (NHS 2018), and three in 1,000 children aged 19 and under (0.3 per cent) have permanent deafness (CRIDE 2017; ONS 2018). This data shows that the great majority of d/Deaf and hard-of-hearing people are adults who have had some previous exposure to sound and a spoken language in their lives. SDH for d/Deaf children needs to be studied and considered as a separate area of expertise to the subtitles provided to adults, because children's exposure to a spoken language and their acquisition of reading skills, depending on the age of onset, take place with a limited and different access to the auditory channel. Before I discuss the characteristics of young audiences, I will examine deafness in its different degrees and in its separate elements, namely amplitude sensitivity, frequency range and spectral detail.

2.3 Deafness

As shown in Figure 2.1, the ear is divided into three parts: the external or outer ear (pinna and ear canal), the middle ear (eardrum, hammer, anvil and stirrup) and the inner ear (cochlea, organs of balance and auditory nerve). The external ear catches sound waves and directs them down the ear canal. These waves cause the eardrum to vibrate. The vibrations are passed across the middle ear by three tiny bones (or ossicles), the hammer, anvil and stirrup, which increase the strength of the vibrations before they get transferred into the cochlea. The cochlea, shaped similarly to a snail's shell, is filled with fluid and contains thousands of tiny sound-sensitive cells, known as hair cells. The vibrations entering the cochlea cause the fluid and the hair cells to move, creating a

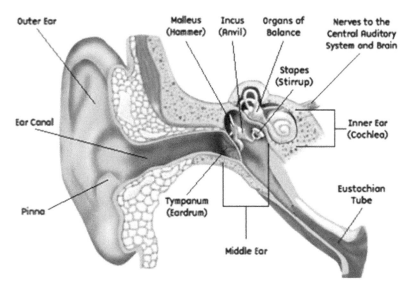

Figure 2.1 Anatomy of the ear. Brian Shannan. 2010. 'Audiology – a curriculum for excellence'. Edinburgh: Scottish Sensory Centre.

small electrical charge or signals that are carried to the brain by the auditory nerve, where they are understood as sound. Deafness happens when one or more parts of the system is not working effectively.

2.3.1 Causes, types and degrees

There are two main types of deafness – conductive and sensorineural; *mixed deafness* arises when both types are present. The main differences lie in which part of the ear is affected, the implications attached to each type, and the reversibility of the former (in most cases) and the irreversibility of the latter.

Conductive deafness results from a fault in the external or middle ear that prevents sounds from passing freely to the inner ear. It is a mechanical problem with the conduction of sound vibrations. It is usually caused by a blockage, such as too much ear wax, a build-up of fluid in the middle ear (glue ear), or an ear infection (otitis). Conductive deafness can also happen as a result of some abnormality in the structure of the external or middle ear, or be due to a perforated eardrum.

Below is an overview of some of the causes of conductive deafness:

- *Cerumen (ear wax) obstruction* denotes a blockage due to the accumulation of ear wax in the ear canal, which impedes the conduction of sound waves; it is common among people of all ages. Hearing can usually be restored with the removal of the ear wax.

- *Otitis media with effusion (OME)* – commonly known as *glue ear* – occurs when the middle ear is filled with fluid that dampens the vibrations of the eardrum and ossicles made by sound waves. The vibrations the cochlea receives are dampened, and so the volume of the hearing is lowered. Glue ear usually occurs in young children, but it can develop at any age.
- *Otitis media* is the most common type of ear infection associated with conductive deafness. It occurs when the middle-ear space becomes filled with fluid (often during a cold), which is sub-sequently infected by germs (bacteria or viruses). It is caused by the inability to ventilate the middle-ear space because of poor functioning of the Eustachian tube (the channel that connects the middle-ear space with the nasal passage). It mainly affects young children (children with glue ear being more prone), but can also affect adults.
- *Otitis externa* – commonly known as 'swimmer's ear' – is an outer ear infection that results in the inflammation of the outer ear canal. Although swimming is not the only cause, the infection is common in children and adults who spend a lot of time in the water, as the moisture can irritate and break down the skin in the canal, allowing bacteria or fungi to penetrate.
- *Otosclerosis* is the result of an abnormal growth of bone in the middle ear which prevents the ossicles from moving freely. It can cause severe conductive deafness that slowly progresses in early adulthood.
- *Cholesteatoma* results from an abnormal collection of skin cells in the middle ear. If left untreated, it can damage the structures of the inner ear, causing sensorineural deafness.
- *Collapse of the eardrum* occurs when excessive pressure behind the eardrum, due to poor Eustachian tube function, causes the eardrum to collapse onto the ossicles, damaging them.
- *Damage to the ossicles* can be caused by trauma, infection, cholesteatoma or collapse of eardrum.
- *Perforation of the eardrum* denotes a hole in the eardrum caused by trauma or infection that affects the performance of the eardrum in capturing sound vibrations.
- *Bony lesions of the ear canal*, that is, growths of bone along the ear canal, can lead to obstruction from ear wax or water.

Conductive deafness is generally temporary and can be corrected with medication or minor surgery. If both treatments prove unsuccessful, amplification with different types of hearing aids is used. The result of this type of deafness is that sounds become quieter, although not usually distorted. According to Tidy (2014), 4 per cent of all school children are affected by conductive deafness.

Sensorineural deafness, also called *nerve deafness*, results in most cases from damage to the hair cells within the cochlea – in the inner ear – and occasionally from damage to the auditory nerve (or both). Age and exposure to loud sounds are the most common causes of deafness. Below is an overview of some of the causes of sensorineural deafness:

- *Presbycusis*: age-related deafness, which occurs when the sensitive hair cells inside the cochlea become damaged or die. It is the most common cause of deafness. Those affected start to acquire deafness between the ages of 30 and 40, and by the age of 80 the deafness becomes significant.
- *Noise-induced deafness*: this results from regular and prolonged exposure to loud sounds (including music). A sudden noise, such as an explosion, can cause a kind of deafness called *acoustic trauma*.
- *Genetic predisposition*.
- *Complications at birth*.
- *Injury to the head*.
- *Viral infections*, such as measles, mumps and rubella.
- *Ménière's disease*, a rare disorder that affects the inner ear, causing vertigo, tinnitus, deafness and a feeling of pressure inside the ear.
- *Acoustic neuroma*, a benign growth on or near the auditory nerve.
- *Meningitis*, an infection of the protective membranes that surround the brain and spinal cord that leads to inflammation and sometimes damage to the nerves and brain. It is common among infants and young children, but adults can also get it.
- *Encephalitis*, a rare but serious condition that causes inflammation of the brain.
- *Multiple sclerosis*, a neurological condition affecting the brain and spinal cord.
- *Stroke*, an interruption of blood supply to the brain.
- *Ototoxic drugs. Ototoxic* means *toxic to the ear*. These drugs are generally used in the treatment of cancer, although they also include certain types of antibiotics.

Sensorineural deafness affects not only the volume of the sound, but also its quality, which is reduced. This type of deafness is in all cases permanent and irreversible, at least at the present time. Seventy-two per cent of the general population of d/Deaf and hard of hearing in the United Kingdom are aged 60 or over. This data confirms that age is the main cause of deafness. Sensorineural deafness in children is mostly congenital or has been acquired perinatally, that is, in the first month of life. A rather low percentage of 0.3 per cent of all school children are affected by sensorineural deafness (Tidy 2014).

Deafness is classified into four degrees – mild, moderate, severe and profound – depending on the loudness of the quietest sound heard, measured in decibels (dB). Table 2.1 lists all four levels, the quietest sound heard in decibels and some simplified implications.

The different degrees denote a loss in *amplitude sensitivity*, that is, a drop in the quantity of the sound perceived – typical of conductive deafness – which can be increased by using a hearing aid to amplify the sounds.

However, reduction in *frequency range* and loss of *spectral detail* are two other factors that characterise sensorineural deafness and denote a drop in the quality of the sound perceived. Frequency is the number of sound vibrations in one second, measured in hertz (Hz). The range of frequencies generally heard by those who are not affected by deafness goes from very low (20 Hz) to very high (20,000 Hz). Most speech sounds occur between 250 Hz and 8000 Hz (JTC 2012). High-frequency deafness occurs when you are unable to hear sounds at the higher frequencies, that is, at frequencies of 2,000 Hz or higher. Examples of these high-pitched sounds are children's voices, the singing of birds,

Table 2.1 Degrees of deafness and their implications

Degree of deafness	Decibels	Implications
Mild	25 to 39	Some difficulty following speech in noisy situations.
Moderate	40 to 69	Difficulty following speech without a hearing aid.
Severe	70 to 94	Use of lip reading or sign language. Cochlear implant.
Profound	95+	Use of lip reading sign or language. Cochlear implant.

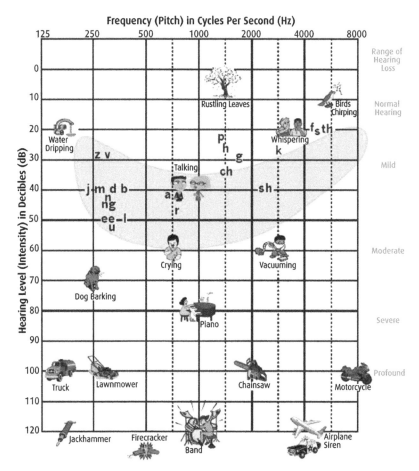

Figure 2.2 Audiogram of familiar sounds by John Tracy Center (https://www.jtc.org/) (JTC 2012)

musical treble sounds, and consonants such as /f/, /h/ and /s/. Low-frequency deafness occurs when you cannot hear sounds at the lower end of the frequencies, that is, at frequencies of 2,000 Hz or lower. Examples of these low-pitched sounds are deep voices, thunder, musical bass sounds, and vowels. Figure 2.2 shows an audiogram of familiar sounds in relation to both loudness and frequency.

Spectral detail is linked to speech intelligibility, specifically to signal clarity in the frequency domain. A deafness demonstrator simulates the effects of these three common consequences of deafness – loss of *amplitude sensitivity*, reduction in *frequency range* and loss of *spectral detail* – in speech, music and noise situations, which can be played individually or simultaneously: see https://www.phon.ucl.ac.uk/resource/hearloss (for Windows only) (Huckvale 2017).

2.3.2 Hearing devices

With the advance of medicine and technology, more solutions to tackle deafness become available. Some of them – namely the diverse range of hearing aids – are relatively unobtrusive, while others – such as cochlear implants and the newest middle-ear implants – require surgery and are irreversible.

2.3.2.1 Hearing aids

A hearing aid is an electronic device that consists of a microphone, an amplifier, a loudspeaker and a battery. It maximises the use of residual hearing by increasing the volume of sound entering the ear. Hearing aids are programmed to match the level of deafness and the ear conformation. An impression of the ear is taken by the audiologist so that the hearing aid fits perfectly.

Hearing aids can be analogue or digital. The latter type allows the user to programme it to suit different environments depending on space, noise level, and the like; they are also smaller and more powerful. The different types of hearing aids include:

- *Behind-the-ear (BTE)*. An earmould is placed inside the ear and connects via a tube to the rest of the hearing aid, which lies behind the ear. This is the most commonly used type.
- *Receiver-in-the-ear (RITE)*. This is similar to BTE but the receiver (loudspeaker) is located within the ear canal and connects to the rest of the hearing aid lying behind the ear with a wire. It is less visible than BTE, but more complicated to use.
- *In-the-ear (ITE)*. An earmould fills the area outside the ear canal, and a small compartment, holding the electronics, is attached to it. It is not suitable for children, whose ears are still growing. It is more complicated to use than RITE and BTE hearing aids.
- *In-the-canal (ITC)*. This is similar to ITE, but smaller. It is not powerful enough for people with severe deafness.
- *Completely-in-the-canal (CIC)*. This is smaller and less visible than ITE and ITC. Because of its size, it can be harder to adjust and remove.
- *Body-worn (BW)*. A small box containing the microphone is clipped onto the clothes and connected via a lead to an earphone. This type

is suitable for those affected by severe deafness, as it is particularly powerful.

- *Bone conduction hearing aid*. This hearing aid, instead of working through air conduction, works through vibration and is generally recommended for those affected by conductive deafness: the microphone picks up the sound, the part of the hearing aid that vibrates is placed against the mastoid bone behind the ear, and sound travels to the cochlea via the mastoid bone. Suitable for those affected by conductive, mixed or unilateral deafness.
- *Bone-anchored hearing aid (BAHA)*. This works similarly to bone conduction hearing aids but a minor operation is required to fix a screw to the skull to which the hearing aid can be attached as required.

The first hearing aid, dating from the seventeenth century, was an enormous ear trumpet with a tube that channelled the sound to the ear. In the late nineteenth century, the acoustic horn, eventually made to fit in the ear, replaced the ear trumpet. It was only at the beginning of the twentieth century that hearing aids became electronic, following Alexander Graham Bell's invention of the electronically amplified sound for the telephone and Thomas Edison's invention of the carbon transmitter, which allowed sounds to be converted into electrical signals, travel through wires and be converted into sounds again at the other end. The first electronic hearing aids were large desktop devices but, as nanotechnology progressed, they became more sophisticated and much smaller. In 1952, the introduction of transistors – switches with two settings, for on or off – revolutionised hearing-aid technology as the number of functions available increased and the size was reduced considerably by using silicon. In the 1990s, digital hearing aids were introduced, which allowed a much more customised use to do with the amplification, reduction, filtration and direction of sound. Today, the newest hearing aid can receive sound wirelessly from telephones, televisions, stereos and computers.

A total of 6.7 million people could benefit from using hearing aids, but only 2 million use them (Hearing Link 2018). According to an international investigation (including Australia, Finland, Sweden, Switzerland, the United Kingdom and the USA) of the reasons behind the non-use of hearing aids, the main causes identified were lack of benefit and discomfort (McCormack and Fortnum 2013). These figures include a large number (80 per cent) of adults aged 55 to 74 who would benefit from hearing aids, but do not use them. Specifically, the study concerning the United Kingdom reported that, of those who had abandoned the use of the hearing aid between eight and 16 years after fitting, only 17 per cent considered that the hearing aid did not improve their hearing, whereas 83 per cent were more concerned with cosmetic aspects, handling difficulties, irritation in the ear and acoustical feedback, which occurs when the amplified sound produced by the hearing aid is picked up again by the microphone, creating a loud sound loop (McCormack and Fortnum 2013).

2.3.2.2 Cochlear implantation

A cochlear implant (CI) is a surgically implanted electronic device that provides a sense of sound to a person who is profoundly or severely deaf. It comprises an external speech processor and an internal implant: the external processor captures sound, converts it to digital signals and sends it to the internal implant, where the signals are converted into electrical energy and sent to an array of electrodes located inside the cochlea. The electrodes stimulate the hearing nerve, bypassing the damaged hair cells, and nerve impulses are transmitted to the brain, where they are understood as acoustic sensations. Cochlear implantation started in the mid-1980s. Implants were first made available to deafened adults and then to deafened children and subsequently to congenitally d/Deaf children. The issue of making cochlear implants available to children born deaf has been extremely controversial over the years.

The Canadian Association of the Deaf makes explicit reference to the ethical aspect of cochlear implantation:

> The Canadian Association of the Deaf-Association des Sourds du Canada is not concerned with decisions made by autonomous deaf adults to have cochlear implant surgery; we recognize that the implants may be of assistance to some adults, particularly those who have been deafened later in life. Instead, we focus on the success rates and ethical dimensions of cochlear implants in young deaf children. (Canadian Association of the Deaf 2015)

It also calls for 'greater scrutiny of the financial profits and marketing schemes of cochlear implant corporations in Canada' (Canadian Association of the Deaf 2015, para. 9) and for full transparency in the dealings exercised by these corporations, provincial health ministries, children's hospitals and auditory-verbal therapy organisations.

The Canadian Association of the Deaf asserts that all deaf children (implanted or not) have the right to acquire sign language (Canadian

Association of the Deaf 2015). Similarly, the British Deaf Association, in response to an article written after the release of *The Silent Child* (2017) film, published on the *Independent* website on 12 March 2018, headlined 'I'm glad The Silent Child is changing the narrative around Deaf children – but it's important to remember that sign language is not the only option', states:

> Lack of early language acquisition has profound consequences for children's development; access and informed choice are imperative. For many parents the opposite is the case when their children are diagnosed as being deaf: the first and only advice they receive is to go for a Cochlear Implant. Never is there the option of bilingualism of both sign language and speech offered.
>
> Surely the best option is that all deaf children can access both BSL and written English and that both languages are respected equally across all fields. (BDA 2018)

The European Union of the Deaf has produced a position paper on cochlear implants in which it is explained that implanted children need to undergo long-term intensive training, supported by speech therapists, to be able to achieve results in the spoken language (EUD 2013). The paper also stresses the necessity of providing parents with balanced information on all the available options, and argues that information on Deaf culture, including sign language – the only language which is fully accessible to d/Deaf and hard-of-hearing children and adults – should be incorporated, concluding that:

> The medical ambition to cure deafness based on a medical model rather than a social model of disability cannot be the only solution especially in view of the UN Convention on the Rights of Persons with Disabilities, which clearly gives deaf people the right to sign language. This must include all children who are implanted, even at an early age to ensure their cognitive health. (EUD 2013)

Only about 5 per cent of eligible d/Deaf adult candidates receive cochlear implants, against 94 per cent of eligible children aged 17 and under (Raine 2013). The small percentage of adults receiving cochlear implants is due to the lack of awareness, among candidates and professionals, both of the criteria for eligibility and of the advantages that can arise from cochlear implantation (Raine 2013). This gap between the numbers of children and adults receiving implants inevitably raises a question as to whether the social, cultural and linguistic pathway followed by the d/Deaf person has an effect on the choice against the cochlear implant made by these potentially eligible d/Deaf adults.

2.4 d/Deaf children

In the United Kingdom, 23.5 per cent of the entire population of 66 million (that is, 15,511,808) are aged 0 to 19 (ONS 2018). There are 53,000 d/Deaf children aged 0 to 19, that is, approximately 0.3 per cent of the entire child population (CRIDE 2017). Around half of them are congenitally deaf, while the other half lose their hearing during childhood, either before or after language acquisition (Action on Hearing Loss n.d.). Deafness that is either congenital or acquired before the child has learned the spoken language is termed pre-lingual, whereas deafness acquired after the child has developed the spoken language is called post-lingual. A child who acquires deafness before learning the spoken language faces communication difficulties that are different from the ones faced by the post-lingually d/Deaf child who has acquired speech with sound, and may, depending on the age at deafness onset, have acquired some reading skills.

Deaf children born to Deaf parents will naturally have a sign language (SL) as their first language and a spoken language as their second language. This is the case, however, with a very small percentage, as 90 per cent of deaf children are born to hearing parents (NDCS 2016). For these children, the communication method is to a large extent chosen by the parents. Since all newborns in the United Kingdom are offered a neonatal hearing screening within a few days of birth, as part of the NHS newborn hearing screening programme (NHSP) introduced in 2006, deafness can be detected early. Generally, for those affected by severe or profound permanent congenital deafness, cochlear implantation soon becomes an option. Implantation for children with permanent congenital deafness is commonly performed by the age of one year (NDCS 2019).

Cochlear implantation was first performed on a child in the United Kingdom in 1987; the child had been deafened as a result of an accident. In 1993, implants became available to congenitally d/Deaf children. The European Association of Cochlear Implant Users reports that nowadays 200,000 children are implanted worldwide (EURO-CIU 2017). In the United Kingdom, 10 per cent of all d/Deaf children (5,641 children) are implanted (66 per cent bilaterally and 44 per cent unilaterally);

of these, 509 children received their implants in the course of one year, 2017–18 (BCIG 2018). The percentage of implanted children indicated by the Consortium for Research in Deaf Education is lower, at 7 per cent (CRIDE 2017). Cochlear implants are made available to individuals with severe to profound sensorineural deafness only, who in the United Kingdom account for 22 per cent of all d/Deaf children (BCIG 2018), which means that nearly half of eligible children currently become cochlear implant users. Other research suggests that approximately 74 per cent of suitable children aged 0–3 years have received cochlear implants and that the percentage increases to 94 per cent by the time they have reached 17 years of age (Raine 2013). Cochlear implants, nowadays, are very much part of the provision for severely (10 per cent) and profoundly (12 per cent) d/Deaf children, but were very controversial in the 1980s and 1990s and still are, to a lesser extent, as discussed in section 2.3.2.2.

Parents who choose cochlear implants for their children are generally opting for an auditory-oral method of communication, in which the spoken language is acquired by learning to listen. The cochlear implant gives d/Deaf children a sensation of hearing and ultimately, with training, children learn to detect and understand the meaning of sounds and to use the spoken language. The auditory-oral pathway is not specific to implanted children as it can also be followed by non-implanted children using hearing aids. In the latter case, children can make use of any residual hearing they may have. The majority of d/Deaf children, 58 per cent, are likely to be using hearing aids because they are not suitable for cochlear implants, given that the degrees of deafness range from mild (for 26 per cent of d/Deaf children) to moderate (for 32 per cent of d/Deaf children). The remaining 20 per cent have unilateral deafness, so they may be suitable for cochlear implantation in one ear only (CRIDE 2017). Figure 2.3 shows a breakdown of degrees of deafness in d/Deaf children.

The way d/Deaf children acquire the spoken language will depend on the method of communication adopted at home and in the educational setting. As shown earlier, most d/Deaf children – 90 per cent – are born to hearing parents and are therefore exposed to a spoken language early on in their lives. When the time comes to choose a school for d/Deaf children, data suggests that 78 per cent of school-aged d/Deaf children attend mainstream schools, 6 per cent attend mainstream schools with a resource provision in place – normally a specialist unit catering for the requirements of d/Deaf children as an integral part of the school –, 3 per cent attend special schools for d/Deaf children, and 12 per cent attend

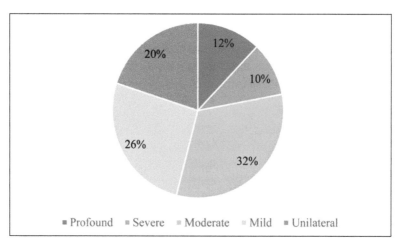

Figure 2.3 Degrees of deafness in d/Deaf children. Source: author

special schools not specifically for d/Deaf children, which may recruit from the group of d/Deaf children with additional health, social or educational requirements, that is, 23 per cent of d/Deaf children (CRIDE 2017). Figure 2.4 shows how d/Deaf children are placed in the educational system.

In the United Kingdom, 67 per cent of severely and profoundly d/Deaf children use a spoken language (English or Welsh) as their only

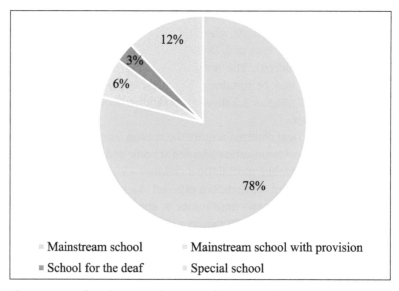

Figure 2.4 The educational setting of d/Deaf children. Source: author

method of communication (CRIDE 2017). Around 28 per cent of severely and profoundly d/Deaf children use sign language of some form in education, made up of 21 per cent who use a spoken language (English or Welsh) with signed support, and 7 per cent who use sign language as their main language (CRIDE 2017). The remaining 5 per cent use a different combination (CRIDE 2017). In the last survey conducted by the Consortium for Research into Deaf Education, the question about the method of communication was narrowed down to children with severe to profound deafness in order to get a better sense of the use of sign language within this specific group of children (CRIDE 2017). Of the entire population of d/Deaf children, 10 per cent use sign language in education (CRIDE 2015). Schools for the d/Deaf adopt a bilingual approach, meaning that sign language and spoken language are used equally in teaching. While the 3 per cent of all d/Deaf children who attend schools for the d/Deaf are clearly exposed to bilingual education, the other 7 per cent of the total who use sign language in education must be using sign language in mainstream settings or in other special schools.

Figure 2.5 illustrates the method of communication adopted in schools by severely and profoundly d/Deaf children. It is clear that the use of sign language and of spoken language with signed support is more common within the group of severely and profoundly d/Deaf children, than in the population of d/Deaf children as a whole, as shown in Figure 2.6.

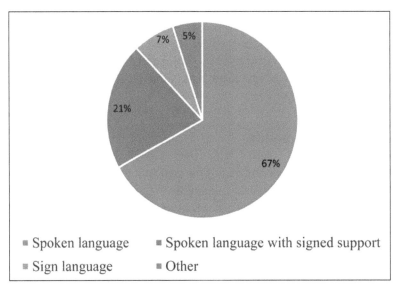

Figure 2.5 Method of communication used by severely and profoundly d/Deaf children. Source: author

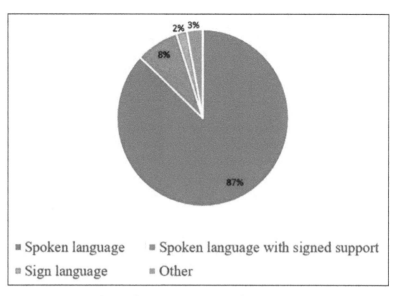

Figure 2.6 Method of communication of d/Deaf children with any degree of deafness. Source: author

The greater use of sign language among severely and profoundly d/Deaf children than in the entire population of d/Deaf children is likely to be the result of the very nature of their deafness. Children affected by mild to moderate deafness have greater residual hearing, which may be maximised with the use of hearing aids, whereas severely and profoundly d/Deaf children who are not cochlear implant users – 12 per cent of the entire population of d/Deaf children, as discussed earlier – would clearly be inclined to communicate using sign language, or at least with some form of signed support.

2.5 Discussion points

2.5.1   Identify organisations in your own country which work for the wellbeing of the Deaf community.

2.5.2   Discuss the different requirements of d/Deaf and hard-of-hearing viewers who access audiovisual materials. How should factors such as method of communication, degree of deafness, treatment option chosen and age of deafness onset guide the accessible solutions offered?

2.5.3   Outline a possible linguistic and sociocultural profile for a mainstreamed deaf child and another one for a Deaf child.

3
Linguistic considerations

Some of the linguistic considerations widely discussed in interlingual subtitling, such as text editing (Gottlieb 1994; Díaz Cintas Orero and Remael 2007; Kovačič 1994), need to be revisited when we produce subtitles for the d/Deaf and hard of hearing audience: the requirements are different because of the limited access to sound of the intended audience. Other aspects important in interlingual subtitling, such as segmentation and line-breaks (Ivarsson and Carroll 1998; Karamitroglou 1998), may be more easily transferred to an SDH or captioning environment. Yet it must be remembered that SDH subtitlers and captioners have to deal with audiovisual, multimodal texts which contain not only dialogue lines but also paralinguistic information, music and sound effects. The following sections address the most relevant linguistic matters encountered in SDH and captioning, and focus on both adults and younger audiences.

3.1 Text editing

The term *editing* covers both omission and paraphrase – that is, eliminating what is not relevant to the comprehension of the message, and reformulating it – and is synonymous with what authors like Díaz-Cintas and Remael (2007) and Kovačič (1994), in the context of interlingual subtitling, call *reduction*. Editing occurs because speech is processed more quickly through hearing than through reading, the activity of reading is combined with watching images, and subtitles are subject to time and space constraints (Díaz-Cintas and Remael 2007). It is particularly required when speech rates exceed acceptable reading speeds, as will be explained in Chapter 4.

When they discuss subtitling for d/Deaf and hard of hearing audiences, Ivarsson and Carroll consider omission of parts of the original

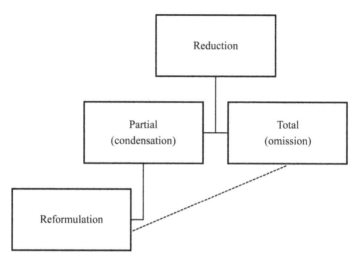

Figure 3.1 Types of text reduction. Source: author

text, rather than paraphrase, to be the ideal technique, since it is less intrusive and less irritating for those able to lip-read (Ivarsson and Carroll 1998). They further point out that omission might also, on occasion, require paraphrase to a certain extent, as, often, omission involves rewriting in order to create proper grammatical sentences, as illustrated in Figure 3.1.

It is important to bear in mind that not all viewers will be able to lip-read, that medium or long shots may not lend themselves to lip reading, and that cartoon characters cannot be lip-read. Nevertheless, mouth movements indicate the start and finish of a sentence, and subtitles that coincide as far as possible with the visuals and the audio are preferred.

Hearing viewers who watch foreign films with interlingual subtitles accept that dialogue is edited to a certain extent. The verbatim-versus-edited issue is peculiar to d/Deaf and hard of hearing viewers, but this is simply to do with the reality that the practice is mainly performed intralingually. From a social perspective, some viewers demand verbatim subtitles as a way of getting the same access to the programme as hearing audiences, but from a practical point of view, the majority of d/Deaf and hard of hearing people have some access to sound, and therefore an accurate transcription of dialogue may be simply easier to follow than an edited one, as the same information is received through the visual and auditory channels. In other words, unedited subtitles may validate what is being heard, while a mismatch between the audio and the subtitle at a comfortable reading speed may be more confusing, and therefore less effective, than a subtitle that has a higher reading speed but tallies with the audio. This is arguably a more convincing argument in support of verbatim subtitles or unedited dialogues than the lip-reading one.

3.1.1 What can be omitted

A number of factors should influence editing choices, namely speech rate in the original programme, age group, complexity of lexis and syntax, amount of information coming through the non-verbal visual channel (such as action-packed scenes) and type of programme.

In considering what elements can be edited out, it is worth bearing in mind that in subtitling there is a switch from the oral to the written mode. In this context, certain features typical of oral discourse, such as repetitions, hesitations, fillers and redundancy, can be partially omitted in the migration to subtitles without affecting the message too negatively. Yet some indications of such features can still be given in the written version, especially if they contribute to characterisation and have diegetic value, that is, narrative meaning.

An example is provided by the fictional character Lauren Cooper, who appears in the British television sketch comedy *The Catherine Tate Show*, aired by the BBC between 2004 and 2007, with two specials in 2009 and 2015. Lauren is portrayed as a bad-tempered and anti-social teenager, who repeatedly and emphatically uses the catchphrase 'Am I bovvered?' as a defensive response whenever she feels offended or embarrassed. In her way of speaking the standard word *bothered* is replaced by the term *bovvered* to convey the th-fronting pronunciation, where the dental fricative /ð/ is pronounced as the labiodental fricative /v/; it tends to characterise people from a low social background. The catchphrase takes other, similar forms, such as 'Do I look bovvered?' and 'Does my face look bovvered?'. Another recurrent pattern characteristic of Lauren's performance is the fact that she delivers her lines at a really fast pace, which, of course, makes subtitling it very challenging. Even though it is frequently repeated, it is unlikely that the expression would be omitted in the subtitles, because of its comedic value. Similarly, imagine that a key figure is being interviewed about a controversial subject and their answers contain hesitations; if these were to be omitted from the subtitles, viewers might get a different perception and think that the speaker is more articulate than they really are. However, omitting hesitations and false starts in contexts in which they result from, for example, a limited command of the language, would contribute to clarity.

3.1.2 Children's programmes

Children's programmes are usually made with hearing, not d/Deaf, children in mind. An attempt at inclusion is made by CBBC, which presents programmes aimed at primary school children aged six to 12 years, and requires that proposals 'consider how different characters and situations might include British Sign Language across our genres' (BBC 2020).

Subtitlers need to think of the requirements of d/Deaf children, which are not necessarily addressed by the programmers. For example, how is new or difficult vocabulary introduced? Theories developed in the field of the second language acquisition of hearing children, which can be transferred to this context, provide evidence that subtitles may facilitate vocabulary acquisition (Neuman and Koskinen 1992) and improve the development of word recognition (d'Ydewalle and Van de Poel 1999; Koolstra, Van der Voort and Van der Kamp 1997; Koolstra and Beentjes 1999).

Subtitles displayed at too high a reading speed and with significant textual volume can discourage children, particularly younger ones, from the whole experience of reading subtitles on screen. While it is important to take into account that viewers may have some, though limited, access to sound and that the subtitles may be fulfilling a didactic role, subtitlers may need to edit dialogue so as to allow for more comfortable reading times. The most favoured and frequent technique of editing in broadcasting is omission, which tends to be applied to difficult words and expressions. Of course, by omitting words, you reduce the length of sentences, and, commensurately, the reading speed can be lowered, as viewers have less text to read. A collateral effect is that children are not exposed to new vocabulary, and hence cannot extend their lexical repertoire. This is why, where possible, subtitlers should attempt to reproduce any repetition of new or difficult words that is present in the soundtrack, and to opt for inclusion in order to encourage the expansion of vocabulary. Other techniques for achieving this aim include allowing longer reading times by delaying the out-time of the subtitle, where possible, and highlighting words through the use of different fonts or colours.

Editing can be an option in the case of narration, which is a technique commonly used in the production of programmes aimed at young children. In other words, narrated speech can be conveyed in the form of dialogue exchanges, for example, so as to decrease the degree of syntactic and lexical complexity, and ultimately the reading speed, of the subtitle. It is true that children are likely to be familiar with indirect speech, as it is commonly found in print; however, as television requires not only reading, but also watching the images and listening, children could possibly gain a clearer picture of the audiovisual programme if subtitles were kept simpler.

For programmes aimed at pre-school children, like the ones on CBeebies, the BBC brand for 0- to 6-year-olds, subtitles could be simplified to the extent of having single words appearing on screen, so that the children recognise the words by shape and sight and associate them with images without necessarily being able to read them. Eye movement research on conventional reading shows that d/Deaf readers have tighter connections than hearing readers between orthography and semantics, that they are extremely attuned to the visual-orthographic make-up of words, and that they quickly detect precise word-form (Bélanger and Rayner 2015).

Moreover, beginner readers learn to read concrete words by sight much faster when the words are connected to images rather than only to their pronunciations (Paivio 2014). At the basis of this approach lies the dual coding theory (Paivio and Lambert 1981; Paivio 1991), which maintains that receiving the same information through different channels promotes and facilitates the learning of a second or foreign language. This theory strongly suggests that subtitles can therefore be exploited as a tool for word recognition, arguably even in the case of pre-school children who are unable to read but may nevertheless be able to associate the shape of the word with the image on screen. Older children with good reading abilities and some access to sound, which most children have nowadays, may find the lack of equivalence between audio and text disruptive. This is why it is important to identify the intended audience when producing the subtitles and captions.

One must remember that subtitles that may appear to be redundant, as they describe what is visually available on screen, still have a didactic function in the case of children's programmes. Some programmes may be more educational than others, in which case the redundancy of text in subtitles – understood as the textual description of actions visually available, or the repetition of uttered words – may have a didactic role if performed deliberately.

3.2 Segmentation and line-breaks

Dialogues are segmented into chunks of text whose extent is constrained by the maximum number of characters available per line and by the maximum number of lines available per subtitle or caption. Generally speaking, there is much more flexibility in captioning than in subtitling. Although captions, similarly to subtitles, are synchronised with spoken utterances and narration, in a place such as a theatre, and depending on the display unit, the spatial and temporal requirements are clearly less strict than those applicable to a screen. Subtitles are generally broken into two (very occasionally three or four) lines, while captions may contain more lines, as they are less likely to obscure the action, a main constraint on screen.

The segmentation of text and the spotting of subtitles – that is, the process of defining the in-time (when a subtitle appears on screen) and out-time (when the subtitle disappears) of individual subtitles so that they are synchronised with the audio, also called *timecoding* or *cueing* – are very important aspects of subtitling and captioning. The main objective is to include a complete idea in each subtitle or caption, whenever possible, in order to improve readability, but always to respect the maximum reading speed that has been set, particularly relevant for subtitles, and to ensure synchronisation between the subtitle or caption, the soundtrack and the images. Viewers have limited memory spans and it is therefore advisable to split complex sentences into shorter ones (Díaz-Cintas and Remael 2007). This is particularly relevant when the viewers are children, as they may be discouraged from reading if there is too much text on the screen.

In my work as a captioner of puppet theatre, the segmentation of text for shows aimed at adults and based on poetry – such as *The Ancient Mariner* by Samuel Taylor Coleridge, *The Butterfly's Spell* by Federico García Lorca*, or *The River Girl* by Wendy Cope – is dictated by the stanzas. Below is an example of a caption from *The River Girl* containing a full stanza, which was displayed for the duration of 16 seconds and at a reading speed of 110 words per minute:

> Beneath the river's smooth and quiet surface,
> Where fishes play and water-weeds unfurl
> In dappled sunlight, lives the lovely Isis,
> Giver of dreams, enchantress, river girl.

When it comes to shows aimed at children and containing poetry – such as *A Child's Garden of Verse*, based on the collection by Robert Louis Stevenson – the stanzas are disregarded in order to avoid captions that are too long and contain too much text. One of the poems featured in the production is *The Butterfly's Ball and the Grasshopper's Feast*, by William

Roscoe. Observe how the opening stanza of the poem is segmented into four captions, as follows:

Come, take up your hats, and away let us haste	90 wpm 04:22
To the Butterfly's Ball and the Grasshopper's Feast;	137 wpm 03:23
The trumpeter, Gadfly has summoned the crew,	127 wpm 03:17
And the revels are now only waiting for you.	90 wpm 04:19

Line-breaks concern the segmentation of text within one subtitle and take into account both linguistic and geometric considerations. From a linguistic perspective, line-breaks should be dictated by semantic and syntactic units, similarly to segmentation across subtitles or captions, and it is advisable to have a greater semantic load in the first line so that the forced break has less impact on the linguistic processing (Díaz-Cintas and Remael 2007; Karamitroglou 1998), as in this example from the puppet show *Joey's Circus Comes to Town*, by Glyn Edwards:

What we want is a fine plan that suits our needs.

There is a contrasting view that advises that in subtitles the upper line should be kept shorter to keep as much of the image on screen free as possible (Ivarsson and Carroll 1998). However, ultimately 'lines should be divided in such a way that words intimately connected by logic, semantics or grammar are written on the same line wherever possible' (Ivarsson and Carroll 1998, 77). In practical terms, article and noun, pronoun and verb, conjunction and clause, and preposition and noun phrase should not be split, if at all possible.

Geometry is also important, and the first and second lines should be as equal in length as possible, because viewers' eyes are more accustomed to reading text in a rectangular than in a triangular format (Karamitroglou 1998). Decisions regarding the length of lines will be further influenced by the nature of the programme. If the programmes are made for the small screen – such as tablets, laptops or even television sets – the different lengths of the lines will not affect the viewing experience as much as they would at the cinema, where a triangular format would require the eye to travel much further owing to the greater dimensions of the screen.

3.3 Non-standard language

The use of non-standard language, that is, of a speech variety that is different in its pronunciation, grammar and lexicon from the standard form of a language, is a common occurrence in dialogue exchanges. Are these features characteristic of speech to be conveyed in written subtitles? Should pronunciation be reflected in the subtitles in the unorthodox way in which the words are spelt (such as *gotcha, kinda, 'em, fella, delish, innit*)?

These questions arise because non-standard forms are not usually seen in writing as much as they are heard. As a result they may require a greater cognitive effort, which may slow down the reading process. This would be the reasoning behind the standardisation of language. However, viewers with access to the audio, even if limited, may find an accurate rendering easier to follow as there will not be discrepancies between what is heard and what is written.

It is important that subtitlers and captioners assess the value that non-standard language carries in any specific context. The way people speak, their colloquial intonation and mannerisms, may be associated with a certain linguistic and cultural background or, in a screenplay, it may be linked to characterisation. If it is deemed meaningful, the subtitler and captioner should remain faithful to the soundtrack and reproduce these words as closely as possible in their written form. It may well be that non-standard language is conveyed, to a degree, to give a hint of characterisation or background while not overloading the viewers with a greater cognitive effort. Alternatively, one can opt for the homogenisation of the oral language used, whereby any departure from the standard register is corrected and neutralised (e.g. *because* is used rather than *'cos, got you* instead of *gotcha* and so on) in an attempt to boost readability.

3.3.1 Children's programmes

When the audience consists of children, subtitles and captions, besides fulfilling the functional role of transmitting the semantic content of what is conveyed by the soundtrack, have the potential to improve viewers' reading abilities and help them build up their vocabulary.

Although some non-standard lexical forms – such as *'cos*, *gotcha* and *kinda* – are colloquial expressions that can be found in most dictionaries of the English language, it is not an easy task for deaf children to recognise them in written form in the short space of time they appear on screen as part of the subtitles. As an example, in the episode 'The Lost Pirates' from *Mona the Vampire* – a cartoon aimed at 6- to 12-year-olds, aired on CBBC – there are several expressions attributed to the speech of pirates, such as *shiver me timbers*, an exclamation used to express surprise, which seems to have originated in comic literature (BBC 2010), and would be rendered in standard English as *shiver my timbers*. It is clear that if the expression was to be standardised, the young viewers would not learn it in its original form. When non-standard expressions are introduced into subtitles, an effort not to compromise readability should be made. If the speech is loaded with non-standard language, only the expressions that are more often repeated in the soundtrack should be conveyed in their colloquial form. Since viewers are more acquainted to reading standard language, the presence of non-standard forms in writing will require a greater cognitive effort. For this reason, it is advisable that subtitles containing non-standard expressions are uncluttered and presented at comfortable reading speeds.

3.4 Orthotypographical conventions

Orthotypographical conventions – the use of upper case, italics, colours and so on – are applied in SDH to represent aspects that are conveyed through the auditory channel: intonation, pauses, interruptions, accents, emphasis, singing and the like.

Not all typographical cues – for example underline and bold – have been adopted in SDH, perhaps because their legibility on screen has not been properly tested. Digital technology allows for the use of different typefaces and sizes in the same programme, but the approach on this front, so far, appears to be rather conservative.

This section initiates a discussion of the orthotypographical conventions normally adopted in SDH, which is continued and elaborated in Chapter 5. At the end of this chapter, Table 3.1 offers a summary and a proposal on the use of these cues.

3.4.1 Upper case

Upper case is used in SDH to indicate emphasis or loud speech (Ofcom 2017; BBC 2019). It may be applied to a single word or a full sentence. For a detailed discussion, see section 5.2.2.1.

3.4.2 Italics

Although there are inconsistencies among broadcasters and streaming services concerning the use of italics, this typographical feature often seems to be employed to indicate genuine off-screen voices – that is, the speaker is not just momentarily off-camera, but is not present in the same space – and voices produced by electronic devices, such as a telephone, television or computer (Netflix 2020a).

These conventions are not internationally applied, however, and vary according to the broadcaster or service provider. The BBC, for example, recommends that in online exclusives, italics, rather than upper case, are employed to convey emphasis (BBC 2019). The use of italics is extended to represent inner thoughts, unfamiliar foreign words, lyrics, and titles of books, films, shows, and the like (Netflix 2020a). When choosing whether to italicise titles or use quotation marks, you should refer to the style guides that apply to general writing.

Given the discordances among the guidelines adopted by broad-casters, subtitling companies and streaming service providers, it is always recommended that you make consistent choices within the same programme or series. Preference should be given to the use of italics for everything that is off-screen (not just momentarily) and unuttered by the characters in the scene: off-screen voices (narration and dialogue lines), sound effects, (background) music, and inner thoughts, including the labels identifying speakers or sound sources.

Italics are also used for foreign words which are not part of the common vocabulary of the target language and to indicate that some accents or pronunciations are reflected orthographically, so as to help the viewers to distinguish terms which are not seen in conventional writing. Many slang terms in urban street talk, such as the British *innit*, a short form of *isn't it*, often used at the end of a statement for emphasis, have become part of official dictionaries, and people have started to get used to seeing them in writing. Other words, such as *izzit*, which is a respelling of *is it* and is commonly used as a response to express indifference, would be obscure if found in their non-standard written form. In such cases, the subtitler or captioner may choose to use italics.

Although no research has been conducted specifically in the field of subtitling on the legibility of italics, respected sources on web content accessibility, such as the World Wide Web Consortium (W3C), advise against the use of chunks of text in italics because they are usually less legible and harder to read (W3C 2016). Italics are commonly used in interlingual subtitling for speech and sounds produced by electronic devices and for song lyrics (Channel 4 n.d.), a practice that has been extended to SDH (Netflix 2020a). Since the speech and sounds delivered through electronic devices are often introduced by an identifying label in SDH, the use of italics, for this purpose, becomes superfluous. The same applies to song lyrics, which are conventionally preceded by a musical note, as discussed in section 3.4.7.

3.4.3 Single and double quotes

In English, two types of quotation marks ('quotes'), or inverted commas, exist: single ('...') and double ("..."). The BBC guidelines suggest that single quotes are employed when the speech comes from an out-of-vision speaker (e.g. in a telephone conversation), who is not identified by a colour, or from a voice-over speaker (e.g. a narrator). Double quotes, on the other hand, are used when the speech comes from a device (TV, radio, loudspeaker) or is a literal quotation of what somebody else has said (BBC 2019).

Other guidelines stay closer to the conventions seen in print. For example, Netflix advises that double quotes should be used for initial quotations while single quotes should indicate a quotation within the initial quotation, following the US English style rules (Netflix 2020a). British English style rules are more variable. Many book publishers use single quotes for initial quotations and double quotes for quotations within quotations (Oxford University Press, Academic Division 2014), but this convention is generally reversed in newspapers.

When there is discordance among the guidelines given, reference should be made to the rules applicable to conventional writing. I tend to agree with Netflix on the use of single and double quotes (Netflix 2020a) and prefer double quotes, as they are more legible on screen than single ones. Double quotes are also to be used for song titles (BBC 2019; Netflix 2020a). In conventional writing, italics are commonly used for titles of books, films, newspapers, and so on. When in doubt, subtitlers and captioners should consistently apply the style guidelines in place for general writing.

If the quotation extends over more than two subtitles, it is advisable to repeat the opening quote in all the subtitles to remind the viewers that the quotation continues, as is recommended in interlingual subtitling (Díaz-Cintas and Remael 2007).

3.4.4 Round brackets

Round brackets – (…) – are used to enclose whispered speech when time and space constraints do not allow the insertion of a descriptive label (BBC 2019). They are also used for asides (BBC 2019). For a detailed discussion, see section 5.2.2.2.

3.4.5 Suspension dots

Suspension dots – … –at the end of a phrase are used in SDH in a very similar way to how they are in conventional writing, to indicate pauses (BBC 2019; Netflix 2020a). The three dots can also appear at the beginning of a phrase to indicate that a subtitle starts mid-sentence (Netflix 2020a). In this book, preference is given to the use of two introductory dots –.. – immediately before the start of a phrase that starts mid-sentence; they are also used to indicate the continuation of an interrupted sentence or the presence of a prolonged pause (BBC 2019). For a detailed discussion, refer to section 5.2.4.

3.4.6 Dashes and hyphens

Dashes (–) and hyphens (-) are conventionally used in SDH to distinguish between different speakers' lines, as discussed in further detail in section 5.1.2.

Hyphens in between letters are used to indicate stammering (BBC 2019), as follows:

> Please, I b-b-beg you.

Some guidelines, like the ones proposed by Netflix, advise that two hyphens (--) be used to indicate abrupt interruptions (Netflix 2020a). While the use of single hyphens between letters to indicate stammering and lengthened vocal sounds – if a character is singing or screaming – is an effective technique, the use of double hyphens is not as immediately clear; it may create some confusion because it is not a conventional punctuation rule and risks not being easily identifiable on screen. Using the three dots – … – for interruptions, pauses and hesitations is recommended.

For a detailed discussion, see section 5.2.4.

3.4.7 Symbols

Some of the conventions used in SDH to convey information that is expressed through intonation are not encountered in print. For example, the symbols **(?)** and **(!)** are employed to express irony or sarcasm, after questions and statements respectively (BBC 2019). For a detailed discussion, see section 5.2.2.

Lyrics in subtitles and captions are often introduced by a quaver – ♪ – to distinguish them from dialogue exchanges, though conventions vary across broadcasters and streaming services, as discussed in section 5.2.2.3. In these pages, it is recommended that all subtitles reflecting lyrics are introduced by the opening quaver, followed by one blank space before the actual text. A closing quaver preceded by a blank space should be inserted in the last subtitle containing lyrics:

Table 3.1 contains a summary of and a proposal for the use of typographical cues in SDH and captioning.

Table 3.1   Orthotypographical cues

Orthotypographical cue	Used for
Upper case	Loud speech
	Emphasis
Italics	Off-screen voices, sound effects and music
	Inner thoughts
	Foreign words
	Accents and pronunciations
	Titles (of books, films, newspapers, etc.)

(Continued table 3.1)

(Continued table 3.1)

Orthotypographical cue			Used for
Quote marks (If the quotation spans more than two subtitles, repeat the opening quote at the beginning of each subtitle.)	Double		Quotations Song titles
	Single		Quotations within quotations
Round brackets (enclosing the phrase)			Whispering Asides
Suspension dots	Closing ...		Interruptions Pauses
	Opening ..		Speech that starts in mid-sentence Continuation of interrupted speech Continuation after a prolonged pause
Dash (at the beginning of the line, followed by a space)			Speaker identification
Hyphens (between letters)			Stammering, lengthened vocal sounds
Symbols	(?) (at the end of the sentence, following a space)		Sarcasm or irony in interrogative sentences
	(!) (at the end of the sentence, following a space)		Sarcasm or irony in declarative sentences
	♪ (at the beginning of each subtitle, followed by a space, and at the end of the last subtitle, preceded by a space)		Lyrics

3.5 Discussion points

3.5.1   Watch this clip from *The Catherine Tate Show*: bbc.co.uk/
         programmes/p008tw11. Identify the challenges if you were to
         subtitle it for d/Deaf and hard of hearing viewers and think
         about how you would edit the dialogue if condensation was
         required.
3.5.2   Watch this clip featuring an interview with Grace Carter (https://
         www.bbc.co.uk/news/entertainment-arts-46739425), analyse
         the segmentation across subtitles and the line-breaks within
         subtitles, and suggest alternative solutions where suitable.
3.5.3   Watch this tutorial on how to add subtitles to YouTube videos:
         https://www.youtube.com/watch?v=_3MMKHqoZrs&app=.
         Then subtitle 'The Lost Pirates' clip from *Mona the Vampire*
         (https://www.youtube.com/watch?v=sCk5m0HObbU,
         starting from minute 12), paying particular attention to the
         rendering of non-standard speech.

4
Technical considerations

4.1 Synchronisation between subtitle and sound/image

Synchronisation is an important aspect of subtitling and captioning. Both sound cues and visual cues, such as a mouth movement, will immediately direct the viewer's gaze to the subtitle or caption area. It is important to remember that deafness very rarely entails a complete lack of access to sound and, in fact, d/Deaf and hard of hearing people will have different perceptions of sounds depending on the degree and type of deafness they are affected by and on the hearing device they use. Synchronisation of subtitles with both sound and image is essential if the viewer is to have an enjoyable experience.

Asynchrony between the sound and subtitles in the form of delays, inherent in live subtitled programmes, is the biggest source of frustration for subtitle users according to the British association Action on Hearing Loss (2018). Unlike in live subtitling, where latency is of the essence, synchronicity for pre-recorded programmes is a variable mainly controlled by the subtitler, except in instances of technical faults in broadcast transmission. Generally speaking, the in-time of the subtitle should coincide with the start of speech and the out-time with the end of the speech segment. Guidelines in the industry agree with this, for instance the ones provided by the BBC (BBC 2019) and by Netflix (Netflix 2020b). However, factors such as reading speed (see section 4.2) and shot changes (see section 4.4) may interfere with these decisions. In exceptional cases, a maximum two-second delay, or latency, between the speech and the subtitle is permitted by the BBC (BBC 2019), while Netflix (Netflix 2020b) is less generous: it allows a time flexibility that varies between three and 12 frames.

The same synchronicity rules also apply to sound effects and music, particularly when working with audiovisual programmes to be shown on screen as opposed to stage performances. Captioning is slightly different in that it does not always feel natural to insert the caption as soon as the music starts. When I launch the captions live, I often feel that it is better to let a phrase of music play before the caption appears. It is probably to do with the different pace found in plays and with the fact that the theatre offers a less constrained context than does a screen. The language of theatre is very different from that of television and even cinema; theatre is an art form delivered live, where scene and lighting changes take place in front of an audience that may not be part of the play, but is present. To a large extent, it is a more immersive experience and the captions will need to blend into the three-dimensional environment of a theatre stage.

4.2 Subtitle presentation rates: reading speeds

There is little common ground among broadcasters and regulators where reading speeds are concerned. While the BBC and Ofcom suggest speeds of 160 to 180 words per minute for pre-recorded programmes (BBC 2019; Ofcom 2017), and up to 200 words per minutes for live programming (Ofcom 2017), Netflix allows greater flexibility, with readings speeds of 20 characters per second, that is, 240 words per minute (Netflix 2020a).

It is important to bear in mind that word length varies significantly between languages. Dutch, German and Finnish, for example, are languages characterised by much longer words than English, so measuring reading speed by the number of characters per second may be more appropriate for accommodating the variation between different languages.

Recent research conducted with hearing viewers suggests that fast subtitle speeds, of 20 characters per second, are preferred to slower ones when the viewers are proficient in the language of the clip. If the language is unknown, slower speeds are preferred, though the researchers do not specify the value (Szarkowska and Gerber-Morón 2018).

Research conducted with regular television subtitle users who are d/Deaf and hard of hearing indicates that subtitles should match the speech in timing and wording, regardless of the rate in words per minute (Sandford 2015). The reason behind this may be that some d/Deaf and hard of hearing viewers will have some access, although limited, to the soundtrack, and they seem to prefer verbatim subtitling at higher reading speeds to edited subtitles where the discrepancies between the audio and the subtitles would be disruptive.

The indications for reading speeds of children's programmes are rather vague. The BBC advises following the speed of speech (BBC 2019), while Ofcom recommends 'heavily edited subtitles' for younger children (Ofcom 2017, 21). Netflix, again, advocates speeds of up to 17 characters per second, which is approximately 200 words per minute (Netflix 2020a).

Besides the target age group, other factors that will influence decisions related to reading speed are the complexity of the lexis and syntax as well as the amount of information coming through the non-verbal visual channel. In other words, if there is a particularly complex sentence or if the screen is packed with action, a more comfortable reading speed may be required. It may just be a matter of anticipating the in-time and/or delaying the out-time of the subtitle by a few frames, without necessarily having to perform any editing on the text. For editing techniques, see section 3.1.

4.3 Minimum gap between subtitles

To enable the viewer to realise that new subtitled content is being presented on screen, it is common practice in the industry to leave at least a 2-frame gap between consecutive subtitles, though some companies may have no gap or go up to 6 frames (Díaz-Cintas and Remael 2007).

4.4 Shot changes

There are two contrasting views on the effect of shot changes on the viewing experience. On the one hand, professional literature on subtitling advises that subtitles should not overrun shot changes, as such an occurrence risks triggering the rereading of subtitles (Ofcom 2017; De Linde and Kay 1999; Baker, Rowston and Lambourne 1984). On the other hand, recent eye movement research suggests that most viewers do not reread subtitles that cross shot changes, though the researchers insist that the experience is disruptive to the viewer's reading (Krejtz, Szarkowska and Krejtz 2013).

On occasion, overrunning shot changes is unavoidable as it is preferable that the decisions on segmentation of text are guided by linguistic considerations rather than by respect for shot changes. Keeping a subtitle within one shot could compromise the presentation of subtitles as complete ideas and, ultimately, their readability. However, to compensate for the visual change generated by the cut, a gap of at least 12 frames between the shot change and the out-time of the overrunning subtitle should be left.

Where possible, subtitles should start on the first frame of the shot and end on the last frame of the shot (BBC 2019). Netflix provides more specific, if convoluted, guidelines by requiring that the in-time is moved up to the shot change, if dialogue starts up to 7 frames before the shot change, and to 12 frames before the shot change, if dialogue starts between 8 and 11 frames before the shot change (Netflix 2020b). Similarly, if dialogue ends up to 7 frames after the shot change, the out-time should be moved to the shot change (respecting the 2-frame gap), and if it ends between 8 and 11 frames after the shot change, it should be moved out to 12 frames after the shot change (Netflix 2020b). This way, the gaps between subtitle times and shot changes are consistently of 12 frames.

4.5 Subtitle layout

The way subtitles are presented on screen is generally decided by broadcasters, DVD publishers, video-streaming operators, film-makers and subtitling companies. With the advent of digital television and the rapid rise of video-on-demand services, users can customise their viewing experience by deciding on the font size, and on some platforms, like Google Play Movie, they can also choose their preferred typeface and background colour.

4.5.1 Font and size

The typeface used on digital television in the United Kingdom, as recommended by Ofcom (2017), is Tiresias Screenfont, designed in 1998 specifically for screen display, with characters that are easy to distinguish from each other. This typeface was adopted following research with blind and partially sighted subjects and d/Deaf and hard of hearing subjects (Silver et al. 1998). The blind and partially sighted people were presented with a sentence printed in (1) Standard AlphaMosaic, (2) Tiresias (first version) and (3) Times New Roman. The d/Deaf and hard of hearing subjects were presented with a short video using a later version of the Tiresias Screenfont typeface, with improvements to the kerning, in four different sizes. The subtitles appeared in white on a black strap at the bottom of the screen. The majority of blind and partially sighted viewers expressed a preference for Tiresias Screenfont, but, unfortunately, no information is reported on the preferences expressed by the d/Deaf and hard of hearing participants in the experiments. Despite its being a popular font in the broadcasting arena, the research basis on which claims have been made concerning Tiresias Screenfont's legibility has been called into question by authors like Clark (2006).

The use of a wide font, such as Tiresias or Verdana, both sans serif (i.e. without extensions at the end of strokes), minimises the risk of unwanted word wrapping, that is, of words in the first line of a subtitle being moved to the second line. This risk occurs because presentation processors (hardware or software that creates a visible rendition of the subtitle file, for example a set-top box or a browser), normally use narrower fonts such as Arial (BBC 2019). Tiresias Screenfont is used for delivery of subtitles on digital broadcasts, whereas for programmes delivered in online platforms, it is recommended that the font is set to a generic proportional sans serif so that the end device uses its default font: Helvetica for iOS and Roboto for Android. The use of non-platform fonts can have a detrimental impact on clarity (BBC 2019).

Users are able to customise the font size on some platforms, such as Amazon Prime Video, Google Play Movies & TV, iPlayer and Netflix. As an authoring requirement, the BBC guidelines recommend that the font size be set to fit within a line height of 8 per cent of the active video height, using mixed upper and lower case, and representing the height of a double-height line (BBC 2019). Again, a wide font such as Verdana is recommended so that lines will not reflow even when processors use a narrower font, which is usually the case (BBC 2019).

While the presentation size of the font for small mobile phones is the unmodified authored font size, for other devices the authored size may be reduced, but not increased, by the processor, which will apply a scaling factor – between 0.6 and 0.8 times the required authoring font size – depending on the device size (BBC 2019).

When legibility is an issue, the subtitler may consider shadowing or contouring the letters, or even inserting a grey or black box behind the subtitles to create more contrast between the colour of the letters and the background.

4.5.2 Number of lines

In broadcast programmes, the maximum number of lines per subtitle should not exceed two, although three lines may exceptionally be included provided that the image on screen is not obscured (BBC 2019, 2009; Ofcom 2017).

For cinema exhibition as well as for DVD distribution and video-on-demand streaming, it is also common practice not to exceed more than two lines per subtitle, with the very occasional three lines.

For live captioned performances, there is more flexibility in the number of lines used, as the available space is not constrained by the screen and images, as further discussed in sections 6.2.3 and 6.2.4.

4.5.3 Line length

In broadcast programmes, the number of characters per line should be limited to a maximum of 37, because of a Teletext constraint, whereas for cinema, DVD and online distribution, the number of characters will be determined by the font chosen, the font size and the width of the letters. In the latter case, the line length is calculated as a percentage of the screen available, that is 68 per cent of the width of a 16:9 video and 90 per cent of the width of a 4:3 video (BBC 2019).

With the advent of digital television, the use of pixels to measure the space occupied by the subtitles makes more sense as characters have different widths; the word 'lit' clearly occupies less space than the word 'mum', although both contain three characters. This new proportional lettering, as opposed to the traditional monospaced approach, allows better use of the space available on screen and can lead to subtitles of some 45 characters per line on certain occasions.

It is common to have 39 characters per line for most languages, 12 to 14 for Japanese and Korean, and 14 to 16 for Chinese on DVDs (Díaz-Cintas and Remael 2014). On video-on-demand platforms, such as Netflix, the maximum number of characters per line is increased to 42 (Netflix 2020a).

4.6 Position of subtitle on screen

Subtitles are generally positioned in the lower part of the screen (Ivarsson and Carroll 1998; Karamitroglou 1998; Ofcom 2017; BBC 2019). This convention is followed in most parts of the world and has been extended to languages which were traditionally written in vertical columns and read from top to bottom, right to left, such as Chinese, Korean and Japanese (Kuo 2017).

The subtitle may be displaced to the top of the screen to avoid covering important information present in the lower part of the screen, such as captions or hard titles (BBC 2019).

Subtitles should be centred on-screen and centre-justified. In the past, positioning was used in broadcasts to identify speakers and therefore subtitles would be left- or right-aligned depending on the position of the speakers on screen, but this practice has been superseded by the use of colours or identifying labels (see Chapter 5, 'Specific requirements').

4.6.1 The safe area

The safe area is the visible area of the video screen where the text will not be cut regardless of the over-scan of the device used. The over-scan is a facility on some devices to adjust the picture size so that the picture is bigger but the edges of the picture are lost. For 16:9 material for UK transmission, the safe area used by most UK programmers is identified as 90 per cent of the active width and 90 per cent of the active height. For certain end credits and for certain programmes distributed internationally, the 4:3 safe area of 67.5 per cent of active width and 90 per cent of active height is required (DPP 2020). The safe area settings can easily be configured in subtitling programs.

The concept of the safe area was an important technical aspect in the past, particularly for broadcast television, because older televisions crop out some of the screen at the sides and can display less of the video outside of the safe area than ones made more recently. Since the advent of digital television, the safe area has lost some relevance, as digital and high-definition televisions do not over-scan images in the same way as older televisions and their frames are rectangular. As far as online players are concerned, the frame size and aspect ratio of the original content are retained so that viewers are able to see every pixel of the frame. However, it is important to bear in mind that cropping can happen in cinemas and that, when watching online streaming, users of video players can resize the video (Brown 2017).

4.7 Subtitle file formats

Most subtitling programs will generate their own subtitling format (such as .w32 for Wincaps and .ezt for EZTitles). Video-editing tools, such as Final Cut Pro and Adobe Premiere Pro, also allow users to create subtitles, as well as to import and export subtitles in a variety of formats, including SRT.

SRT (SubRip text) is the format most commonly used to export subtitles; it allows very basic text formatting, derived from HTML tags for bold, italic, underline and colour. Most processing applications do not support HTML tags (one that does is Subtitle Creator). This is clearly an issue in respect of subtitles for d/Deaf and hard of hearing audiences. However, the SRT format, which is supported by most video players and distribution platforms, may work well in a context in which colours are not used and in which the formatting choice of typeface, font size, and use of shadowing, contouring or blocks can be decided at a later stage, during viewing, potentially by the viewer, as is the case with VLC media player, for example.

SSA (SubStation Alpha) is a more complex subtitle format than SRT formatting that supports text formatting and karaoke-style animation; its improved version is ASS (Advanced SubStation Alpha). These subtitle formats are native of the open-source tool Aegisub and are frequently used in anime fansubs.

Some formats derive from subtitle standards, as is the case with WebVTT (Web Video Text Tracks) (.vtt), designed by the World Wide Web Consortium (W3C). Based on SRT, this format may be more appropriate for subtitling and captioning for d/Deaf and hard of hearing people, as it allows additional formatting options, including the allocation of colours to identify speakers. WebVTT is widely used in the Web community and is supported by browsers, YouTube and Vimeo, but not by Facebook.

XML-based subtitle formats are commonly used in broadcast television and in the film industry. They come in different formats, such as TTML (Timed Text Markup Language) and DFXP (Distribution Format Exchange Profile). TTML is based on a standard developed by W3C, and DFXP includes three profiles that derive from TTML, that is, the presentation profile for video players, the transform profile for video editing, and the full profile which includes all the features defined in the TTML standard. This explains why TTML and DFXP are often treated as synonyms.

EBU-STL (European Broadcasting Union Subtitles) is a legacy standard, used in broadcasting. It is a binary format and cannot be edited with a text editor. EBU-STL's successor is EBU-TT (European Broadcasting Union Timed Text), a modern XML-based format. The EBU-TT format is based on the TTML standard, but is specifically tailored to be more suitable for use with broadcast video and Web video applications. EBU-TT-D, used for the distribution of subtitles over IP-based networks, enables the best possible control over styling and placement, supporting responsive design, that is, automatically optimising the look for different screen sizes.

These formats can only be opened and edited using professional subtitling software not available as freeware.

This section has offered a discussion of the most commonly used subtitle file formats, but there are many more that have not been included. A good starting point for identifying subtitle file extensions and compatible programs is https://www.file-extension.org (accessed 10 September 2020).

4.8 Discussion points

4.8.1   Read this article on fonts in Design Shack magazine: https://designshack.net/articles/typography/best-font-for-subtitles, and this one by accessibility consultant Joe Clark: http://screenfont.ca/fonts/today/interim. Compare the views expressed and find points in common.

4.8.2   Using a subtitling program of your choice – including freeware such as Aegisub, Subtitle Edit or Subtitle Workshop – subtitle a clip of your choice applying the technical parameters specified in this chapter. Save the file in a format of your choice.

4.8.3   Open the subtitle file created in the previous activity – or any subtitle file – using different players, such as Quicktime, RealPlayer and VLC. Verify whether there are any differences in the way the subtitles appear to the viewer.

5
Specific requirements

5.1 Speaker identification

The voice indicates to hearing viewers who is speaking. This is not always accompanied by clear visual information, in cases where, for instance, the shot is long, the speaker is off-screen or there are multiple characters speaking simultaneously. For d/Deaf and hard of hearing viewers, their limited access to audio calls for speaker identification.

Depending on the medium, different techniques may be used to identify speakers, ranging from the use of colours to identifying labels and dialogue dashes.

5.1.1 Colours

On broadcast, and consequently in broadcaster video-on-demand platforms (BVOD), colour is the favoured technique for speaker identification (Ofcom 2017; BBC 2019), although we may still come across positioning as a technique for identifying speakers when old subtitle files are used. The BBC specifies the use of four colours: white, yellow, cyan and green, in order of priority. The narrator is conventionally allocated yellow. Colours should be used consistently throughout the programme; if there are more characters than colours, the same colour can be allocated to more than one character as long as they are not in the same scene. Green is described as a 'floater', that is, available for more than one minor character as long as they do not appear together in the same scene (BBC 2019).

It is interesting that in broadcasting the colours chosen are the ones traditionally used in analogue television despite the availability of a myriad of colours in the current digital era. Although this may be as the result of re-using files that were originally created for analogue television, the reality is that there is a marked lack of research on experimenting with the use of new colours that do not compromise legibility.

In captioning puppet theatre, I use colours to identify speakers in productions which are aimed at older children, whereas in productions aimed at younger children I use icons, as discussed and illustrated in section 6.2.2.

5.1.2 Labels and dashes or hyphens

Labels and dashes are commonly used in DVDs, VOD and at the cinema to identify speakers or to distinguish between two speakers who appear in the same subtitle, the use of dashes being a convention commonly used in interlingual subtitling. Since there are no stylistic guidelines that have been adopted at an international or national level, standards vary widely, meaning that the following variations, among others, may be used, depending on the broadcaster or language service provider. For the purposes of this book, the preferred variations are enclosed in boxes.

To identify speakers, descriptive – e.g. **[WOMAN]** – or nominative – e.g. **[ALICE]** – labels may be used. The variants in layout in use are presented below. The last two examples are taken from the BBC (2019) and Netflix (2020a) respectively:

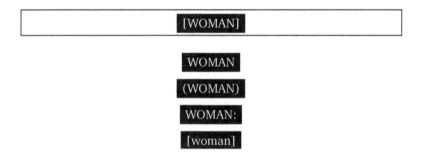

The other option for indicating that the text belongs to different characters is to precede each of the lines with a dash (–) or a hyphen (-), in which case a space may or may not follow the dash or hyphen that appears before the dialogue:

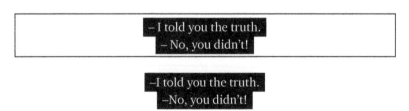

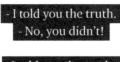

The first example, with a dash followed by a space, reflects the BBC recommendations (BBC 2019), while the last one, with hyphens and no spaces illustrates the Netflix ones, which do not exclude the insertion of a label after the hyphen if further identification is still needed (Netflix 2020a). As this last convention risks cluttering the subtitle, it could be argued that if there are multiple speakers in one subtitle and identification is required, labels should be used rather than dashes.

In theatre, Stagetext uses the name, written in capital letters, followed by a colon and two spaces before the dialogue, presumably for clarity, as shown below:

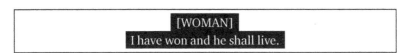

When captioning puppet theatre, I use labels to identify speakers in most adult productions. The identifier is written in upper case within square brackets and above the actual text, as shown in the example below from *The Ancient Mariner* by Samuel Taylor Coleridge:

[WOMAN]
I have won and he shall live.

The choice of square brackets and upper case for all elements that are specific to captioning is rooted in the belief that readers can easily distinguish them from dialogue. Round brackets would also be acceptable if it were not for the fact that they are traditionally used in broadcasting to indicate whispering.

5.2 Paralinguistic features

Paralinguistic features, in this context, are those non-verbal vocal elements that may have communicative value and may need to be subtitled or captioned for the d/Deaf and hard of hearing audience. Some paralinguistic features (such as accents, pronunciation and intonation) are expressed through verbal sounds and some others (such as laughter, cries, groans, grunts, snorts) are expressed through non-verbal sounds. In the classification of these features, Poyatos's analysis and classifications are particularly relevant (Poyatos 1993, 2008).

5.2.1 Accents and pronunciation

When an accent is relevant to the plot, the subtitler or captioner will need to include this information. This is in line with the recommendations put forward by the BBC (2019). Subtitlers and captioners will need to use their judgement to make decisions about what it is pertinent to include. Let us imagine a news scenario where passers-by are being interviewed about climate change. The interviewees, especially if the report comes from a diverse capital city, may have different accents. However, since this information is irrelevant in this particular context, it does not need to be included in the subtitles. On the other hand, there are cases where the indication of an accent or pronunciation is crucial to the enjoyment of the programme. Think for instance of *The Catherine Tate Show*'s 'Translator' sketch, aired on 27 October 2006 on the BBC (https://www.youtube.com/watch?v=XY66ZJ0TFUI&t=6s), in which character Helen Marsh convinces her boss that she can be the translator (more accurately the interpreter) for a meeting of international executives from seven countries. What follows is an emulation of the stereotypical sounds and rhythm of the languages she 'translates' into, including exaggerated nasal sounds for French, a repetition of the Spanish voiceless dental fricative /θ/ found in words like Barcelona, and so on. The comic effect would be completely lost if the various pronunciations were not indicated in the subtitles. In this particular case, rather than using a generic, explicative label like [repeats the sound 'th'], an orthographic transcription of the sounds would be more appropriate so as to convey those stereotypical sounds of the languages in question. As an example, the Spanish could be rendered thus:

Th, th, th, th, th, th, th...

When I captioned the puppet show *The Butterfly's Spell* by Federico García Lorca, which was based on an official English translation of the original play and had been recorded by Spanish actors, I deemed it relevant to indicate that the narrator had a Spanish accent. I then decided to caption it by means of a label, as it was not necessary to indicate what the Spanish accent sounded like:

> [SPANISH ACCENT]
> Ladies and gentlemen:
> The play you are about to hear
> is of no great consequence,
> and yet, disturbing.

The BBC, similarly to the names tag, prefers the following variant:

> SPANISH ACCENT:
> Ladies and gentlemen:

Variations in the pronunciation of words may be dictated by social considerations. For example, the phenomenon of t-glottalling – the replacement of /t/ with a glottal stop in a word – is stereotypical of British urban speech and is associated more commonly with younger than with older speakers, and with informal settings. The glottal stop is phonetically indicated as /ʔ/ but it is frequently represented orthographically by an apostrophe,'. As an example, the word 'better' could be pronounced as /ˈbɛʔə/, which is often orthographically represented as 'be'er'. Elon Gold addresses this linguistic mannerism in one of his stand-up comedy acts (https://www.youtube.com/watch?v=9oDjrvIqeIs), and without a representation of this pronunciation in the subtitles, the comic value of the clip would be lost. This is a clear example of when the pronunciation needs to be represented orthographically to achieve the intended goal of the original, as below:

> There are two ts in the word "le'er"
> and yet they're nowhere to be found.

However, in a context where young Londoners are being interviewed by a news reporter, representation of the phenomenon of t-glottalling may be completely irrelevant.

It is worth bearing in mind that reading the words with an indication of their pronunciation is not something we normally do, so it may require some extra reading time.

5.2.2 Intonation

'Intonation is primarily a matter of variation in the pitch level of the voice, but in such languages as English, stress and rhythm are also involved' (Encyclopaedia Britannica 2015). Intonation conveys the attitudes and emotions of the speaker, and signals the difference between statements and questions. While the latter can be represented by punctuation, relevant expressive meanings exclusively conveyed by voice need to be indicated for d/Deaf and hard of hearing viewers. Intonation is more closely related to verbal elements than other paralinguistic features which convey emotions but are not strictly connected to words (such as groaning, grunting, snorting) or are more closely related to actions (such as coughing, laughing and crying). In Poyatos's classification of non-verbal communication, qualifiers are non-permanent features of the voice (Poyatos 1993, 2008). For example, a voice can be harsh, tense or sarcastic and words can be whispered, sung or emphasised, depending on the context and the situation. In all cases, we are dealing with how words, rather than sounds, are being uttered. The following sections take a closer look at how these paralinguistic features are conveyed in subtitles and captions.

5.2.2.1 Emphasis

Loud speech expressing emphasis or shouting is traditionally indicated in SDH through the use of upper case, as in the following examples:

> That wasn't me, it was HIM.

> HELP!

Because most of what we read is in mixed case, reading upper case is harder than reading lower case, so this orthotypographic device should be used sparingly (BBC 2019). If a whole sentence is shouted, a label at the beginning of the subtitle is preferable to writing the whole sentence in upper case:

> [SHOUTS]
> I have had enough of you and your family!

It is also important to bear in mind that, more often than not, emphasis is visually conveyed through bodily actions and that, even in cases where the speakers are off-screen, the content of the subtitle or caption may still express it.

Some guidelines discuss the use of italics rather than upper case to convey emphasis, such as the Ofcom ones (2017). The BBC guidelines also consider the use of italics, but only for online exclusives and as an experimental solution, since there is little research available to support its effectiveness (BBC 2019). I tend to agree with the Netflix recommendations for the use of italics (Netflix 2020a), which, rather than being used to indicate paralinguistic features, are reserved for off-screen voices.

5.2.2.2 Whispering

The BBC guidelines say that whispered speech, when it is not conveyed visually, should be indicated by the use of a label (BBC 2019):

WHISPERS: It's a secret.

I would like to suggest that instead of the format recommended for the label by the BBC, i.e. upper case followed by a colon, upper case within square brackets and without colons should be used consistently for paralinguistic elements that are specific to subtitling for d/Deaf and hard of hearing viewers:

[WHISPERS] It's a secret.

Another device for conveying whispering, but one less favoured by the BBC guidelines (2019), is the use of round brackets to enclose the whispered words:

(Don't tell anyone.)

The advantage of using round brackets rather than labels is that they have less effect on the reading time, though their meaning may not be so clear. To complicate matters further, round brackets can also be used to represent asides. Whichever the decision taken for a particular programme, it is important that the chosen technique is applied consistently.

5.2.2.3 Lyrics

The conventions for indicating lyrics vary from enclosing each subtitle that contains lyrics in quavers (♪) (Netflix 2020a) to starting each subtitle that contains lyrics with a hash mark (#) and having a closing hash mark only after the final lyrics subtitle (BBC 2019). Nowadays, the use of the hash mark should be avoided, as it is an arbitrary convention that dates back to the analogue era when more appropriate symbols such as the musical note were not supported by Teletext. The BBC guidelines recommend the use of beamed notes (♫) for their online content only (BBC 2019), thus displaying different conventions depending on whether the programme follows a traditional broadcast or is archived in their online repository. Below is an example of how the lyrics present in the puppet show *A Christmas Carol* by Charles Dickens were captioned:

> ♪ God rest ye merry, gentlemen,
> Let nothing you dismay,
>
> ♪ Remember Christ our Saviour
> Was born on Christmas day
>
> ♪ To save poor souls from Satan's power,
> When we were gone astray.
>
> ♪ O tidings of comfort and joy. ♪

As illustrated, an opening quaver has been inserted at the beginning of all captions containing lyrics and a closing quaver at the end of the last lyrics caption to indicate the end of the song.

Note that lyrics are stylistically treated as poetry, so, for example, the first word of each line may be capitalised. While the conventional punctuation and orthography rules applicable to prose may not be strictly followed, the use of commas and full stops should be consistent.

In terms of textual editing and reading speed, lyrics constitute an exception. Unlike dialogue exchanges, they can be left unedited even when the reading speeds are higher than the intended maximum. In the case above, 'God rest ye merry, gentlemen' is a well-known Christmas carol, which means that editing it down is not an available option: it would be inaccurate and untrue to the song. Observing the technical rules applicable to speech – such as the maximum six-second duration of subtitles on screen or their display rate – is not recommended, as they may have a negative impact on rhythm, for example, which is particularly important in the case of songs.

In line with the BBC guidelines, subtitlers and captioners will need to use their judgement and perform some editing, if required, in cases of unknown songs written specifically for the programme, where the value of the content might be comparable to that of speech (BBC 2019).

5.2.2.4 Sarcasm

The use of sarcasm in speech is distinguished by the inflection in the voice but it is also largely dependent on context. Figure 5.1 is an example from the cartoon *Arthur*, showing the convention followed by the BBC, which consists of adding **(!)** or **(?)** at the end of the sarcastic sentence, depending on whether the sentence is exclamatory or interrogative (BBC 2019).

Sarcasm may be conveyed by the content of the subtitle itself as well as by the context. In Figure 5.1, Arthur is on his own thanking Buster, who is not present, so the sarcasm may be inferred without the need for a typographical cue such as **(!)**.

In cases where an indication is required, the following layout is recommended: the insertion of an exclamation or question mark within brackets, following the statement or question, leaving a space before it to assist legibility:

That's so generous of you (!)

Are you feeling OK (?)

5.2.2.5 Other voice qualifiers

While the primary qualities of a voice, such as pitch (degree of highness or lowness), are intrinsic characteristics (Poyatos 1993, 2008), subtitlers and captioners may need to qualify non-permanent features of a voice. When it is deemed relevant, the quality of the voice, rather than the emotion, should be subtitled or captioned. Besides being loud, whispery or singing, a voice can be tremulous, abrupt, muffled, mumbling, and so

Figure 5.1 Typographical cues for sarcasm. Source: author

on. These qualities often, although not always, convey an emotion. For example, a tremulous voice may indicate nervousness, a monotone voice may suggest tiredness, while a muffled voice may be the result of something covering the speaker's mouth. It is preferable to find adjectives that evoke an emotion and let our viewers make their own inferences rather than provide subjective interpretations.

These features should be subtitled or captioned when the professional considers them important and they are conveyed exclusively through the voice, without any visual reference. The usual format applies:

> [ABRUPTLY] Excuse me.

5.2.3 Vocal non-verbal sounds

These sounds are produced by a human voice, are non-verbal and can be linked to actions – such as coughing, crying, laughing, whistling, sneezing and gargling – or to emotions not directly reflected in the action – such as grunting, groaning and sighing.

The use of the simple present tense or present participle to subtitle sounds follows conventional grammar principles. More exactly, if a sound is produced in one go, then the simple present is used, but if the sound has a continuous longer duration, then the present participle is required. As an example, a speaker can react to something with laughter, in which case the subtitle or caption would be:

> [LAUGHS]

If the speaker is laughing and speaking at the same time, the present participle is used:

> [LAUGHING] Stop it, this is
> so hilarious, I can't get over it.

When the source is undefined, it may be more appropriate to use a noun:

> [LAUGHTER]

> [CRYING]

Some of these sounds may have a corresponding orthographic transcription in the form of an interjection – hmm or hm for humming or hesitating, ah for sighing, ha for laughter, and so on. When they are followed by speech, such a transcription may be less disruptive than a label:

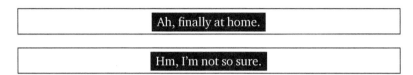

Some words are onomatopoeic, that is, they are similar to the noises they refer to. Onomatopoeic words may be favoured for programmes or shows aimed at young audiences, but they may not always be appropriate in programmes and shows tailored for adults, as they carry a playful connotation associated with comics. Think how the following subtitles or captions may fit a cartoon but not be suitable for a drama for adults:

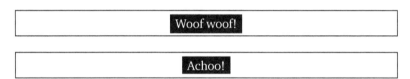

In programmes aimed at adults, the corresponding descriptive labels, respectively 'barks' or 'barking' and 'sneezes' would be preferred.

It is also worth bearing in mind that in programmes aimed at children, redundancy between image and subtitle or caption may have a didactic function. For example, it may be obvious that the cow is mooing, because the information is visually provided, but the subtitler or captioner may nevertheless choose to indicate it in a subtitle or caption to perform a didactic function and help the children to build their vocabulary:

[COW MOOS]

Note that breaking away from the convention of using upper case for all elements specific to d/Deaf and hard of hearing viewers should be considered, specially when the programmes are tailored to younger audiences. Lower case is easier to read because the letters have a more distinctive shape than upper-case letters and because of the greater exposure we have to it, which leads to our not having to 'read' the word, as the meaning may be instantly recognised from the familiar shape of the group of letters:

> [Cow moos]

5.2.4 Pauses and hesitations

Pauses are conveyed through timing in speech and punctuation in written texts. Three dots (...) appear at the end of a subtitle or caption to indicate an interruption or prolonged pause, while two dots (..) are inserted at the beginning of the next subtitle or caption to express the continuation of the paused sentence, as shown in the example below (BBC 2019):

> I was thinking that...
>
> ..we should escape.

Some guidelines do not advise using introductory dots for prolonged pauses, but would contemplate the use of three introductory dots to indicate that a subtitle starts mid-sentence (Netflix 2020a). I think that the two dots, not employed or needed in conventional writing, are effective if used consistently to indicate the continuation of an interrupted sentence, a prolonged pause, or a subtitle or caption that starts in mid-sentence. When watching programmes on a screen or at the theatre, viewers are likely to be exposed to other visual input and the two introductory dots act as a link to textual information previously seen or indicate that the beginning of the sentence is missing.

Often a pause is accompanied by hesitation, in which case fillers such as er or um would be inserted to indicate them, like this:

> Er, I wouldn't say that because it's,
> er, just not fair.

If there is a pause within a subtitle, the three dots should be resorted to. Note that the BBC guidelines advise against leaving a space after the dots (BBC 2019), but for clarity, a space should be inserted after the dots, as below, in line with Netflix's guidelines (Netflix 2020a):

> I think they've named her... Marta?

To conclude, with the exception of the two introductory dots, in subtitles, pauses and hesitations are generally conveyed through the application of conventional writing rules and punctuation.

5.3 Music

Captioners and subtitlers need to make music accessible to d/Deaf and hard of hearing audiences. It is my contention that the importance of instrumental music is generally underestimated, perhaps because there is a misconception that d/Deaf and hard of hearing audiences do not enjoy music. This does not happen with lyrics, discussed in section 5.2.2.3, because they are verbal.

Deafness should not preclude people from enjoying and accessing music. With their captions and subtitles, professionals must address two types of audience: people who had full access to music through hearing in their lives before becoming d/Deaf or hard of hearing, and also those born profoundly d/Deaf, who, incidentally, can become musicians or dancers, just the same as hearing people. This is the case with Deaf dancer Chris Fonseca (https://www.youtube.com/watch?v=lBBpAu 9LCN0) and Danny Lane, artistic director of Music and the Deaf (http://www.matd.org.uk). They are two among many who consider music to be a universal language. Music is absorbed and processed in a very individual way and it involves much more than hearing, as explained by deaf percussionist and composer Evelyn Glennie, who considers the body to be a resonating chamber experiencing sound (https://www.ted.com/talks/evelyn_glennie_how_to_truly_listen).

When I started subtitling as a freelancer, in 2008, the guidelines on how to subtitle instrumental music were non-existent or quite vague. A subtitling company for which I was subtitling American television series instructed me to simply insert the tag [music] whenever there was music playing in the background. One of the main changes to have taken place in the last 10 years is that subtitlers may be granted more freedom on this aspect, as companies admit that the research on the subtitling of music is rather limited and therefore tend to be less prescriptive and more open to suggestions from subtitlers with expertise in the field.

While d/Deaf and hard of hearing viewers may perceive music in a different manner from hearing viewers, there is not one way of subtitling music for this audience, as it is very diverse and includes people with different onsets and degrees – ranging from profound to mild – of deafness, and different hearing devices, namely cochlear implants and hearing aids. Despite the heterogeneity of this audience, subtitlers and captioners will endeavour to find solutions that address their different requirements.

Professionals still need to assess whether the music in each particular case is relevant and therefore needs to be subtitled or captioned. It is not the role of the subtitler to account for all the auditory elements present in the soundtrack, as new subtitlers have a tendency to assume. Of course, discerning what is relevant is not an easy task, and an inability to do so results in the insertion of subtitles that, rather than supporting the viewers to enjoy the programme or the play, distract them from it. Less is often more.

Looking at the bigger picture is a good way to start. For example, if we think of different cinematic genres, we will find that the music in horror films has a different function from that in comedies. In horror films, it is used to provoke emotions, often fear, in the viewers, while in comedies it may act as a filler. Before we even start to discuss how to subtitle or caption instrumental music, we know that the importance of music subtitles in a horror film is greater than in a comedy.

I often wonder whether the effect provoked by listening to suspenseful music could be replicated in written form through a subtitle or caption. This question is particularly pertinent in the case of wordless puppet shows that are entirely performed to music, and the decision to make them accessible through captioning can be a challenging one. In all these instances, I opted against captioning the plays, because the music was intended as accompaniment. In other words, the shows were already accessible, without a soundtrack. So why would I ask my audience to read a caption which tries to point to the mood of the music when this same mood is also conveyed by the movement and actions of the puppets? I deemed it unnecessary, and perhaps even intrusive, to force my audiences to take their eyes off the characters on stage to read a caption that would only validate the mood of the scene.

But then again, if artistically I choose to have a soundtrack rather than silence, why would I deprive my audiences of the opportunity to access it? The final choice is often influenced by the communicative resources in place. I chose not to caption the wordless productions because I am of the opinion that the mood of the piece is expressed more effectively through the actions and movement alone. A textual visual representation of the music would detract from the enjoyment of the action on stage. In this case, the cognitive effort required to read the caption(s) would not be justified, as the information provided in writing would be redundant.

However, if assistive tactile technology was available, I would choose to use it to enhance the experience. Some people struggle to hear high-pitched sounds, such as voices, while others experience difficulty in hearing low-pitched sounds, like the bass. In these cases, vibrations can be an important dimension of the perception of music by d/Deaf and hard of hearing people.

One of the earliest innovative solutions for enabling music to be experienced in a tactile way is the Emoti-Chair, developed in 2008 at Ryerson University in Toronto, Canada. Based on the model human cochlea (MHC) and using 16 vibrating motors, it enables music to be experienced through the skin rather than the ears. The ear has tens of thousands of mechanoreceptors capable of differentiating sound frequencies, whereas the skin has only four mechanoreceptors responding to different forms of touch. The ear can distinguish between frequencies in the range 20–20,000 Hz, whereas the skin can only distinguish frequencies below 1,000 Hz. This limitation was addressed by lining the back of the chair with voice coils so as to allow the users to distinguish frequency through spatial positions rather than relying on the mechano-receptors (Holland 2015). The Emoti-Chair is the predecessor of tactile audio displays (TADs). A spin-off of Ryerson University, Tad Inc. (https://www.tadsinc.com) is a research and development company whose main objective is to make sound in films and music more accessible to d/Deaf and hard of hearing audiences. Nowadays, it provides tactile audio displays ranging from portable home and office systems to immersive gaming systems.

Technology also offers inclusive music and dance solutions for d/Deaf and hard of hearing people, such as portable engineered dance floors with embedded transducers which transform sound into vibrations (https://feelthebeat.dance/the-technology). Events such as Sencity (https://www.sencity.today/en) provide accessible music experiences in which all senses are stimulated. The music is not only perceived through a vibrating dance floor – Sensefloor – but through taste and smell too.

Another assistive solution is the vibrating backpack made available to members of the audience for performances captioned via Stage-sync. SoftLab at Universidad Carlos III de Madrid, Spain, developed this automated system for closed captioning and offered its audiences the possibility of experiencing the music in a multi-sensory way. For further details on Stage-sync, see section 6.1.2.

Despite the great potential promised by these technological solutions, a downside is the fact that these systems are not regularly available in cinemas, theatres or other venues, but can, most likely for financial and logistic reasons, only be enjoyed at one-off events.

Music can be represented visually in the conventional way, that is, by relaying it through written text. Once the subtitler or captioner has decided that the music in a particular scene is relevant because it describes a mood or adds to the enjoyment of the programme, a decision needs to be made as to what to include in the subtitle or caption. Let us start by looking at subtitling and captioning instrumental music using text only. At the opening of the puppet show based on *A Christmas Carol* by Charles Dickens, the curtain goes up to reveal Scrooge sitting at his desk to music specially composed for this show. The caption – which appears in italics to indicate that the music is heard in the background and is not being played in the scene – may fulfil the function of setting the mood:

> *[MELLOW PIANO MUSIC]*

The inclusion of the name of the instrument in the descriptive label is often advised, so as to give an indication of the quality of the sound. It is better to choose adjectives that describe a pace or a mood than to use subjective, generic adjectives such as beautiful. The pace can be rapid, slow, fast, while the mood can be eerie, sinister, ominous, playful, epic, ethereal, and so on. Depending on the programme and the target audience, it may be appropriate to use musical terms such as crescendo, fanfare and mid-tempo.

Below is an example from the puppet show *Mr Rabbit Meets Brer Santa*, by Movingstage Marionette Company, in which Brer Rabbit, the central character in Joel Chandler Harris's stories, dances to specially composed music:

> *[JAZZY UPBEAT MUSIC]*

Notice how information about the mood and genre can prevail over the detail of the instruments being played.

In the film *School of Rock* by Richard Linklater, there is a clear switch in the soundtrack from classical to rock music. Students are playing classical music in class. Shortly afterwards, we see Dewey, the fake supply teacher, fetching instruments from his van. At this point, there is a clear and relevant music change: the type of music can be indicated as well as the title of the song and the name of the performing artist:

> *[ROCK MUSIC:*
> *"SUNSHINE OF YOUR LOVE" BY CREAM]*

Later on in the film, we see Dewey and the students playing famous rock songs. At this stage, there is no need to reiterate that the musical genre is rock, as this is already conveyed by the context; however, it is important to include information such as the title and artist, as shown in the example below. Note that the subtitle is not italicised because the music is scene-bound, that is, it is being played on screen, not as background music:

["HIGHWAY TO HELL" BY AC/DC]

A conscious effort needs to be made by new subtitlers and captioners to avoid including information about the music that is already being conveyed visually. As an example, if someone is playing the piano on screen, this should not be subtitled as 'plays the piano', as that information is redundant and can appear patronising to the viewers. Instead, information may be included about the piece that is being played.

Instrumental music can be conveyed in the subtitles without the need for words, by using icons to represent instruments and musical notes for rhythm, as seen in the discussion of captioning for younger viewers expounded in section 6.2.2. Unfortunately, there is a discrepancy between the potential offered by technology and what is actually supported by existing subtitling software, which is confined to textual input and a very few symbols, like the quavers used to indicate the presence of music. This may change in the future if academics, practitioners and software developers initiate collaboration in an attempt to explore new and creative practices. Until then, those willing to experiment with non-textual input will need to rely on software that is not designed for subtitling and captioning, such as PowerPoint or Keynote, which makes the process much more time-consuming and not financially viable.

There are other ways of representing music in a non-textual manner, through sound waves for instance. This can be achieved mechanically through the use of cymatics, which, in practical terms, consists of placing a Petri dish filled with liquid on the cone and dust cap of a speaker. The audio frequencies of the music played will create a visual pattern by moving the liquid (https://www.youtube.com/watch?v=MwsGULCvMBk). Another cymatics visualisation can be produced by sprinkling sand on a metal plate and making the plate vibrate, for example by drawing a violin bow along the edge. The higher the frequency, the more complex the patterns produced will be, as illustrated in this video (https://www.youtube.com/watch?v=GtiSCBXbHAg). This method could work particularly well in a live performance.

Music visualisation can also be achieved electronically, using amplitude and frequency as input properties. The output can vary from a representation that simulates an oscilloscope display (https://www.youtube.com/watch?v=dnJyOIixvhQ) to more elaborate ones (https://www.youtube.com/watch?v=J2YQD8Go_Hc). The animated imagery can be produced using specific visualisation software, such as Atari Video Music and MilkDrop, or more generic media player software, such as Windows Media Player and QuickTime Player.

Musician, inventor and software engineer Stephen Malinowski has developed the Music Animation Machine (http://www.musanim.com) with the purpose of creating animated graphical scores. Although his work (https://www.youtube.com/user/smalin) cannot be replicated, as he uses software written by himself that is not available to the public, he has published a Windows software program that turns MIDI files into animations and can be downloaded from http://www.musanim.com/Player.

5.4 Sound effects

Sound effects are diegetic (i.e., they take place within the world of the film or play) artificially reproduced sounds – other than dialogue exchanges, music and paralinguistic elements – aimed at creating a dramatic effect in an audiovisual programme or play. Sound effects can be produced by different sources, including people and animals, but they are non-vocal, as opposed to the vocal non-verbal sounds which would be classified as paralinguistic features discussed in section 5.2. Because sound effects may have storytelling value, we generally need to caption and subtitle them. However, if they are conveyed visually, the caption and subtitle may become redundant. In this sense, an off-screen gunshot will most likely need to be subtitled, whereas it would be unnecessary to subtitle a gunshot that can be identified on screen. An iconic scene that serves to illustrate this point comes from the film *Bambi* (1942) (https://www.youtube.com/watch?v=7sCqMEkgLIw), in which the young fawn Bambi and his mother run away from the hunters and the audience can hear – but not see – a thunderous shot. In the next scene, Bambi appears calling his mother but there is no reply. That off-screen shot is a crucial moment in the plot and needs to be subtitled.

There are exceptions when it may be appropriate to subtitle or caption sounds that could potentially be seen on screen. In the film *Dracula* (1931), the scene in which Renfield arrives at Count Dracula's castle and the great door of the castle creaks open is a case in point. The sound associated with the action of the door opening contributes to the haunting atmosphere, so this requires a subtitle. One could further argue that the viewer would not expect to hear the creaking sound from a door opening, which adds to the setting. If the source of the sound is not immediately recognisable, the following subtitle could be used:

> [DOOR CREAKS]

The format recommended by the BBC is the presentation of the subject followed by an active, finite verb (BBC 2019), as shown in the above example. If the source is undefined, we can use nouns or present participles instead, as in the following instance, where the use of italics indicates that the sound is off-screen:

> *[FOOTSTEPS]*

Similarly to paralinguistic features, if the programme is aimed at young children, the subtitler and captioner may prefer to use onomatopoeias instead of descriptive labels, to maintain the playful tone and make reading fun. For example, instead of 'car horn', we could choose the following solution for young children:

> [BEEP BEEP]

If we were given the freedom to be more creative, we could even indicate the source of the sound by adding an image of the car in the form of an icon, as discussed in section 6.2.2.

5.5 Silence

It may seem counterintuitive but, on occasion, we may need to subtitle filmic silence, which is generally used in the most suspenseful sequences in a film. Consider, for example, how silence is used as a vehicle for storytelling in the iconic scene in *Raging Bull* (1980) (https://www.youtube.com/watch?v=Z0lt-Qougws) that precedes the violent defeat of Jake LaMotta. It could be indicated as follows:

> *[SILENCE]*

In this instance, italics are used to indicate that the silence relates to the character's inner feelings rather than to actions in the scene.

Silence is particularly important in the film *The Artist* (2011), which starts as a silent film accompanied by music. Sound is first introduced in a dream sequence in which silent film actor George Valentin is in his dressing room, and as he puts his glass down, a clink is produced (https://www.youtube.com/watch?v=1qvNfSwTAfE). This is the first occurrence of sound, which is followed by several others produced by objects and people, while George Valentin is mute. There are no fixed rules about subtitling sounds and silences, but a good starting point for subtitlers is to assess the intention of the director and to evaluate the diegetic meaning of silence and sounds. As an example, the clinking of the glass, despite being a clearly visible sound, will need to be subtitled as the film until now has been silent. Later on in the scene, should the subtitles indicate that George Valentin is unable to utter sounds or is this clearly conveyed through the images? The viewers may infer this information through the visuals – the actor's repetition of actions accompanied by an increasing frustration – but for the purposes of immediacy, the insertion of one subtitle when the actor makes his first unsuccessful attempt to utter sound, may be helpful. This could simply be indicated as follows:

[NO VOICE]

In this example, we are being specific, but the following subtitle could be an alternative:

[NO SOUND]

The expression [MOUTHS], which is commonly used in SDH, is never an ideal solution as mouthing does not denote a sound but rather an action that can be seen on screen. 'Inaudible' or 'indistinct', in contexts in which the speech is muffled, are suitable alternatives, as they are directly connected to sound.

5.6 Discussion points

5.6.1   Watch *The Catherine Tate Show*'s 'Translator' sketch with the Amara subtitles (https://amara.org/en/videos/wmauzTuS8s Qw/info/catherine-tate-the-offensive-translator). How are paralinguistic features dealt with?

5.6.2 Watch Elon Gold's stand-up comedy act (https://www.youtube. com/watch?v=9oDjrvIqeIs), identify the subtitling challenges and find solutions as to how the jokes can be successfully conveyed through subtitles.

5.6.3 Watch the video *How Deaf People Enjoy Music* (https://www. facebook.com/watch/?v=10155585526449220) and make a list of the aspects of deafness and music that may not occur to a hearing person, to be used as guidance for future subtitling and captioning projects.

5.6.4 Watch this clip from *School of Rock* (https://www.youtube. com/watch?v=yMvpJDbWX_c&t=7s) and consider how you would subtitle the first four minutes. Compare your choices with the subtitles in Appendix 3.

5.6.5 Download the Music Animation Machine MIDI Player (Windows freeware) (http://www.musanim.com/Player) and a MIDI file of your choice from https://www.midiworld.com. Play the file and explore the different types of available animations.

5.6.6 Discuss the official subtitles of the '[barking continues] [ringing continues]' clip from *The Artist* (http://readingsounds.net/ chapter6).

5.6.7 Visit the following sound glossaries and find more sources of this type that could be useful in your SDH or captioning practice:

- Sounds made by people: https://www.macmillandictionary. com/thesaurus-category/british/sounds-made-by-people;
- Sounds made by animals: https://www.macmillan dictionary.com/thesaurus-category/british/sounds-made- by-animals;
- Sounds made by object: https://www.macmillandictionary. com/thesaurus-category/british/sounds-of-things-hitting- or-rubbing-together.

6
Captioning theatre
and subtitling live events

6.1 Captioning theatre plays

The work of subtitlers and captioners is generally linked to the post-production stages of film-making and theatre-making. Nevertheless, authors such as Romero-Fresco advocate the integration of accessibility as part of the film-making process (Romero-Fresco 2013). In the theatre world, there are examples of collaborations between academics and theatre-makers, such as Integrated Immersive Inclusiveness (https://immersivetheatrecaptions.wordpress.com), a project that explores the development and use of immersive technologies to support further development of integrated inclusiveness for d/Deaf and hard of hearing audiences in small-scale touring productions. The project engages the touring theatre company Red Earth Theatre, pioneers of integrated theatre, and researchers from the University of Nottingham working on immersive technologies.

Other examples of inclusive immersive theatre that embed accessibility from the beginning of the creative process are provided by Deafinitely Theatre (https://www.deafinitelytheatre.co.uk) and Graeae Theatre Company (https://graeae.org), both placing d/Deaf and disabled artists centre stage. The inclusiveness promoted by these companies is intrinsic to their nature. An ideal development would be that their practices – which include the use of sign language and creative captioning, among other things – start to be integrated into mainstream theatre.

A collaboration with the film-makers or dramatists at the early stages of production may be crucial to rendering a film or a play accessible to d/Deaf and hard of hearing audiences. Minor adjustments in production may make all the difference. Let us imagine there is a relevant sound, for example an off-screen gunshot, that is intrinsic to a scene but occurs just before a shot change and lasts less than a second. Extending the duration of the shot by a few frames may allow for the insertion of a subtitle that is not disrupted by the shot change. First-hand examples from my work at the Puppet Theatre Barge are discussed in section 6.2.

Captions, similarly to SDH subtitles, give people who are d/Deaf, deafened or hard of hearing access to live performances. Open captions consist of text displayed on or near the stage which are aimed at making the play or event accessible to d/Deaf and hard of hearing audiences. The text can be likened to opera surtitles to some degree, as it includes dialogue lines and lyrics, but is characterised by the presence of non-verbal auditory elements that are specifically aimed at d/Deaf and hard of hearing audiences, that is, speaker identification, intonation, accents, sound effects and music.

Closed captions, unlike open captions, are not screened to the entire audience but are made available through devices designed for individual use, ranging from smartphones and tablets, to handheld devices provided by the venue, small screens installed on the back of the seat in front, often in a designated area of the auditorium, and even special glasses.

6.1.1 Open captioning in theatres around the world

In the United Kingdom, the main provider of open captions is Stagetext (http://www.stagetext.org), founded in 2000 by Peter Pullan, Merfyn Williams and Geoff Brown, all three affected by deafness. Their first ever captioned performance, of the Royal Shakespeare Company's *The Duchess of Malfi*, took place on 15 November 2000 at the Barbican Theatre, in London. Pullan explains the motivation behind their project: 'Theatre is about being involved in the development of the characters and being emotionally and intellectually attached. I feel deprived of this great experience' (Peter Pullan, quoted in Stagetext n.d.). Stagetext supplies the captioning equipment to theatres across England and has trained theatre captioners, who have been accredited with the Stagetext Certificate in Theatre Captioning for Deaf People. As a more cost-effective solution, and in order to be able to afford more captioned shows, theatres may decide to purchase their own captioning equipment; in such cases, Stagetext will train local people or staff at the venue. There are currently approximately 40 theatres and production companies in England that have their own captioning equipment and in-house Stagetext-accredited theatre captioners. Figure 6.1 shows the caption unit in relation to the stage in the play *Les Liaisons Dangereuses* at the New Vic Theatre, in

Figure 6.1 Stagetext caption unit at the New Vic Theatre's production of *Les Liaisons Dangereuses*, July 2007. Source: Robert Day, photographer

Newcastle-under-Lyme. In an ideal scenario, the caption unit should be positioned so that it can be seen by everyone and as close as possible to the actors' head height.

In big theatres, a caption unit may be placed on either side of the stage, as in the case of *Top Girls* by Caryl Churchill at the National Theatre in 2019. Audience members sitting in the middle of the auditorium may have found it difficult to follow the captions. The play in itself is particularly challenging, as it is characterised by fast, overlapping dialogue lines: perhaps a screen above centre stage closer to the actors, as in Figure 6.1, would have helped. However, the choice against such an arrangement may have been dictated by the requirements of the lighting or the moving of scenery.

Stagetext was involved in the launch of a captioning service in Scotland, which has been run by the Federation of Scottish Theatre (https://www.scottishtheatre.org) since 2007. Arts & Disability Ireland (ADI) (http://adiarts.ie) has been captioning in the Republic of Ireland since 2007, while Theatre and Dance NI (https://theatreanddanceni.org) has provided captions to theatre and production companies across Northern Ireland since 2011.

Theatre Development Fund (TDF), a not-for-profit New York-based organisation dedicated to making live theatre and dance accessible to a broad and diverse audience, offered its first captioned theatre performance in London on 28 March 2000. Working closely with theatre captioner Donald DePew, the founder of c2 (http://c2net.org), they presented an open-captioned performance of the Royal Shakespeare Company's production of *Antony and Cleopatra* at the Barbican. c2 is internationally recognised as the pioneering authority in open captioning, with over 800 theatrical productions at more than 180 venues in their records (TDF 2020).

In Spain, Teatro Accesible (http://www.teatroaccesible.com) works similarly to Stagetext, but also audio-describes plays for blind and partially sighted people. Of more recent inception, having been set up in December 2011, Teatro Accesible has made accessible 508 plays in 119 theatres across 49 different cities (Teatro Accesible 2020). Figure 6.2 shows a typical set-up for a captioned performance.

In Australia, The Captioning Studio (https://captioningstudio.com), founded in 2004 by Nari Jennings and Alex French, is the only provider of open and closed captions for the arts and live events. Venues have the option of using TV screens for open captioning, or smartphones and tablet devices via the GoTheatrical! app for closed captioning.

Providers of open captions, such as Stagetext, are generally concerned about delivering a service that is fully inclusive, raises people's awareness of deafness and does not require the user to collect special equipment or sit in specially equipped seats. In this respect, having closed-captioned solutions alongside open-captioned events is an

Figure 6.2   Teatro Accesible caption unit by Aptent. Source: Aptent

improvement, as it increases the options offered to d/Deaf and hard of hearing audiences. The risk is that as closed-captioned solutions become more available, theatres and venues will adopt them in preference to open captioning. If they do, we will end up with events that are more accessible than inclusive.

6.1.2 Closed-captioning solutions in theatres

In recent years, a number of closed-captioning solutions have become available to d/Deaf and hard of hearing audiences. One of the most revolutionary developments in the United Kingdom is the automation of the cueing of the captions introduced, in conjunction with the smart-caption glasses designed and manufactured by Epson,[1] into all National Theatre (https://www.nationaltheatre.org.uk) productions since February 2019. This development is the culmination of a four-year collaboration between the National Theatre and a team of speech and language experts led by Andrew Lambourne. The main innovation introduced with the smart-caption glasses is the triggering of automated captioning, based on artificial intelligence technology, for which the live captioner is no longer required, so that costs can be reduced.

The precursor to this project was CaptionCue, a venture funded by Nesta, the Arts and Humanities Research Council and public funding by the National Lottery through Arts Council England, and coordinated by Stagetext involving the National Theatre, the University of Roehampton and Screen Systems. The aim of the project was twofold. First, to develop and use existing speech-following software (SFS) to output captions automatically. The software used for CaptionCue was a phonetic speech-follower that followed the rhythm of speech at a phonetic level and could deal, to a certain extent, with deviations from the script. Secondly, the project tested the reception of the captioned performance to different types of display devices: an LED screen integrated into the set, an LED screen at either side of the stage, and tablets. The results showed that audiences were generally satisfied with the quality of the captions, despite noticing that the captions were not always fully synchronous with the dialogue. In terms of attention divided between the action on stage and the captions, the LED screens at the sides worked better than the LED screen integrated into the set,while the least satisfactory in this respect were the tablets, as more time (52 per cent) was spent on the captions and less on the stage (43 per cent) (Stagetext 2015).

The system developed for the smart glasses is a custom-created speech recognition system which correlates the words uttered by the actors with the script, the arrival times of sound and lighting cues, and the duration of events, with a metadata-enhanced script (associated with stage events in the live performance), so as to create a live timecode (determining the in-times and out-times of the captions). The timecode is used to trigger and broadcast pre-prepared captions live onto the smart-caption glasses over the wi-fi. The glasses have a handheld controller that allows viewers to personalise their experience by adjusting the font size, the colour, and the number of scrolling lines (from one to three) per subtitle.

I visited the National Theatre on 21 June 2019 to test the smart glasses, but on this occasion some of the captions were unfortunately out of synchrony. Luckily, that night the performance was being open-captioned too, so access was still available to the d/Deaf and hard of hearing audiences despite the infelicitous technical glitch. The day after, Tabitha Allum, of the National Theatre, explained at the National Association of Deafened People (NADP) conference that the issue had been caused by a faulty wi-fi connection. The National Theatre was built in 1976 and the building was constructed in a way that is not compatible with wi-fi technology, so the technical team had a challenge to address. Despite the mishap on the day, the potential offered by this state-of-the-art technology is very promising: I encourage those who can to pay a visit to the National Theatre to attend a performance and request the glasses (https://www.nationaltheatre.org.uk/your-visit/access/caption-glasses) so that they can have an in-person experience that will help them to understand better how technology is enriching this field.

Figure 6.3 illustrates the experience of reading captions through the smart glasses. For some, the glasses offer the best means of presen-tation, since the LED screen used for open captioning, often perceived as intrusive by hearing audiences, is no longer required, and d/Deaf and hard of hearing audiences no longer need to switch their attention from the drama unfolding on stage to the captions on the screen. Using the glasses, the captions appear to hover in space wherever the user is

Figure 6.3   Smart glasses. Source: author

looking. The distraction element often associated with open captions, from the point of view of hearing theatregoers, is also removed.

Automated caption triggering came into the picture as a potential means of reducing the costs of manual cueing. The first stage of the project consisted of recognising and classifying the content types present in a play, in order to create metadata to accompany the caption script. Sound effects, songs and music, and pauses are all used as information to guide the automated caption triggering. Primarily, the caption cueing is triggered by speech: when the system recognises that the next expected utterance has started, the caption is triggered. Sound and lighting cues are also used, and for recorded effects or songs the timing is used, as it is for the expected duration of pauses. All this additional information helps to reduce the uncertainty inherent in automatically following speech in a theatre environment where there are other sounds, variable clarity or quality of audio, and changes in the simultaneity of speech and the way actors deliver lines.

The dialogue from the script and the additional metadata are fed to the voice-following software. The software follows the audio from the performance in real time and adjusts the running-caption cueing time accordingly, using also sound and lighting cues. As the actors utter their lines, the software recognises them and automatically cues them by referring back to the fed script. If actors forget their lines, no caption will appear. If they go slightly off script or improvise, the lines will not be captioned and the system will get back in synchronisation when a good match is received. The speech-following software developed for the smart glasses does this much more accurately and reliably than CaptionCue. It is also more able to deal with extraneous noise or with the system getting slightly out of synchrony.

The main challenge of automated caption triggering is dealing with mismatches between what is being uttered and what has been fed to the system. At present, the automated delivery of the captions would benefit from greater human assistance, such as a live captioner ready to intervene in situations which are not satisfactorily resolved by the automated system, for example improvisation by actors. However, since automated captioning was introduced to reduce the costs of manual cueing, such a possibility is unlikely to be contemplated by many theatres.

The smart glasses were showcased by Leeds Playhouse in 2019, and more recently some cinema exhibitors have shown an interest. In January 2020, the London Short Film Festival hosted four screenings at which the smart glasses were made available to audiences at the British

Film Institute (BFI) in South Bank, so that the first UK pilot in cinemas could be conducted.

An ongoing research project conducted by the Galician Observatory for Media Accessibility (GALMA) (http://galmaobservatory.webs.uvigo. es/projects/captioning-glasses-for-the-national-theatre) is investigating the reception of closed captioning at the National Theatre using a new prototype of Epson smart glasses. Specifically, the aspects being looked at are the quality of the automated captions, the experience of the users wearing the glasses and their overall impressions. If the results obtained are positive and encouraging, the smart glasses may have a future in interlingual theatre captioning too.

Another example of automated captions comes from Spain, where SoftLab at Universidad Carlos III de Madrid developed Stage-sync, using artificial intelligence, deep learning and advanced audio processing. Captions, Spanish Sign Language and audio description can be accessed through the GoAll application on personal mobile devices. The experience is complemented by a vibrating backpack that members of the audience can request in order to get a multi-sensory experience of the music. The downside is that a change of pace in the delivery of speech, a pause or applause can de-synchronise the captions. The server tracks the place in the script, and is able to do so by gathering information from experience of other performances. The application premiered in 2017 with the musical *The Addams Family* (https://lafamiliaaddams.com/adaptado. html) in Spain and has since expanded to Brazil and the United States.

Another closed-captioning solution is Difference Engine, a tool developed by Talking Birds (https://www.talkingbirds.co.uk) that gives access to captions through the use of personal mobile devices. Figure 6.4 shows Difference Engine in use at *The Female Warrior* by Talking Birds, in the gardens of St John's House Museum, in Warwick. The captions, in this case, are not automatically cued but are operated onsite from a laptop by someone from the creative team who knows the show's cues and understands pacing. This solution is popular with small-scale or site-specific companies, but has also been adopted by some more established theatres – such as Southwark Playhouse and the Young Vic Theatre – and festivals, such as Manchester International Festival. The script is imported onto the Difference Engine system, where it is divided into captions and altered as required. It is possible also to switch into a live captioning mode, which is often used for post-show discussions or unscripted parts of a play. At the moment, this is performed by the operator, who types the text live, using a normal keyboard.

Figure 6.4 The Difference Engine set-up by Talking Birds. Source: Talking Birds

Closed captioning certainly promotes accessibility, but does not have the element of inclusiveness offered by open captioning. It is a solution fairly invisible to other audience members and one that requires the user to make special arrangements, such as collecting the device on arrival at the theatre, holding it throughout the performance, or sitting in a designated area in the auditorium. It is interesting to note that the Difference Engine is described as a 'discreet new tool', a definition that suggests that discretion is somehow desired (Talking Birds n.d.). Nevertheless, closed-captioning solutions increase the options available to d/Deaf and hard of hearing theatregoers, who can choose whether to attend any performance, availing themselves of closed captions, or to attend one of the few open-captioned performances offered per run. Let us hope that theatres will keep and increase their commitment to offer open-captioned performances, so that the choice given to the audience is even wider.

6.1.3 The role of the theatre captioner

At Stagetext, the main provider of captions in the United Kingdom, theatre captioners start working on the production approximately four weeks before the captioned performance. An up-to-date script will be received, and formatted according to the captioning conventions taught on the training course, using the specific subtitling software provided. An aspect that Stagetext feels strongly about is that the text should be captioned verbatim. Sound effects, music and paralinguistic features (accents, intonation) are included alongside dialogues, narration, poetry and songs (Stagetext 2019b). The theatre captioner works with the script and a DVD recording of the show, and is also expected to attend at least two rehearsals, besides liaising with the stage manager to clarify any aspects that are intrinsic to the production. The preparation of the captions takes approximately 60 hours. In the case of open captioning, the preparation work culminates in the captioned performance, which involves live cueing. At this point, the theatre captioner will need to make decisions mainly related to timing. Because of this, open captioning entails a commitment that starts when the script is received and ends with the captioned performance. Aspects such as the positioning of the caption unit may be discussed by Stagetext's theatre programme manager directly with the venue.

In performances at which closed solutions are used, the role of the theatre captioner ends with the delivery of the captions to the venue. In the case of the glasses at the National Theatre, the cueing of the captions is done automatically and the presence of the theatre captioner is not required, while the solution offered by the Difference Engine system requires the cueing of the captions to be done live, similarly to how it is done in an open captions setting. Interestingly, the theatre captioner who prepares the file may be part of the creative team and the cueing may be performed by the stage manager, the director, the producer, or even a volunteer. The delivery, in this case, does not require specific technical skills but rather someone who knows the production and understands pace. No guidelines are provided by Talking Birds, the inventors of the Difference Engine, who give only instructions on how to create the captions script from a technical and logistical point of view and advice on how to include sound and music descriptions. They are keen on theatre-makers using their creativity, although they signpost good practice (e.g. Stagetext) and suggest that those who have no experience in the field engage a theatre captioner who does.

6.2 Captioning puppet theatre

I have worked as a puppeteer at the Puppet Theatre Barge since 2007. During that time, I started my research on subtitling for d/Deaf children, which led me to a greater involvement and commitment to accessibility and inclusiveness. I had an urge to put into action what I was learning about rendering spaces accessible to d/Deaf and hard of hearing people. The Puppet Theatre Barge became the one space where I had all the cards in place to create accessible and inclusive performances. The captioning service was launched in October 2016. By that time, I had worked as a puppeteer in a great number of productions, which was extremely helpful, because not only was I familiar with the soundtracks of the shows, but I also had a real understanding of puppetry as an art form.

One of the characteristics of this specific puppet theatre is that the soundtrack is recorded before the actual show. This allows the captioner to pre-prepare the captions (using a subtitling editing program such as Wincaps), synchronise them to the audio – in the same way in which subtitlers synchronise the subtitles to a video – and simply press 'play' at the beginning of the show in replay mode. This is one method of captioning the performance at the Puppet Theatre Barge. Another way of doing it is by cueing the captions live, which would be mandatory in a situation in which the sound is live. In my case, live cueing is required when I wish to introduce features into the captions that are more creative than those conventionally applied, and so are not supported by the subtitling software, such as icons. On occasions like these, I use Apple Keynote (or its equivalent, Microsoft PowerPoint). It sometimes happens that I am engaged to work as a puppeteer for a run of shows, which lasts approximately two months. In such cases, the captions would be in a more conventional format and automatically launched. I would keep the laptop backstage to check that the system is running correctly.

Besides working as a puppeteer and captioner at the Puppet Theatre Barge, I make puppet shows and have my own touring company, String Theatre (https://www.stringtheatre.co.uk). Without my having consciously decided to make them so, all the productions I have made so far – except for one that contains poetry – are wordless and intrinsically accessible to d/Deaf and hard of hearing audiences. I have developed an interest in forms of immersive theatre and am considering introducing visual text as part of the productions.

I think that being a puppeteer and in a close relationship with the creators of the shows benefits my captioning practice because there is a mutual understanding. As a captioner, I may be struggling to describe a piece of music present in the show. I can easily get hold of the writer of the show and ask what the intention behind the choice of that particular music was. I may even be provided with a script containing the directions given to the musical director. Similarly, the close relationship established with the puppeteers allows me to request that minor but meaningful changes be implemented for the captioned performance. For example, in productions where a fair amount of fog is used, I may request that the output of fog is limited if the visibility of the captions is compromised.

As a puppeteer, I can understand the artists' intentions. Often, visual effects are created with the use of lighting, props and perspective. To give an example, there is a piece of scenery which we call the rain curtain; it has plastic strips hanging from a baton. The way the scenery is operated and lit allows the artists to create the illusion of rain. If there is dialogue, and therefore captions, and the rain is in view, the visual effect is destroyed by the projector's light beam. A possible solution to this problem is to strike the rain curtain before the appearance of the captions, a minor adjustment which will preserve the quality of the production.

6.2.1 The Puppet Theatre Barge

The Puppet Theatre Barge (https://www.puppetbarge.com) is a 50-seat marionette theatre on a converted barge in London. The theatre presents puppet shows for children and adults and is moored in Little Venice for most of the year and in Richmond-upon-Thames during the summer. The theatre was founded in 1982 by Gren and Juliet Middleton and is a family-run business. Most of the shows presented are in-house productions, although occasionally visiting companies are received.

It specialises in long-string marionettes, meaning that the puppeteers stand – out of view – on a bridge, and the marionettes are the main and only characters on stage. Often the productions combine marionettes with shadow puppets. While most shows are aimed at families or adults, the company has a couple of productions in its repertoire aimed at children aged three to eight years. These shows are performed with rod puppets, that is, puppets which are operated from below through the use of rods. The puppeteers are still out of view.

The type of puppetry and the target audience affect captioning decisions – such as text overload and the choice of techniques to identify speakers and convey music, sound effects and paralinguistic features – as well as logistics. To give an example, in marionette productions the captions appear at the top of the stage and there is flexibility in the number of lines used, while in rod productions the captions appear below the stage and the number of lines is limited to two.

Figure 6.5 Puppet Theatre Barge auditorium with caption unit. Source: author

The venue is equipped with a fully functional induction loop which surrounds all the seats in the auditorium, meaning that d/Deaf and hard of hearing audiences do not need to reserve specific seats for the performance. Figure 6.5 offers a view of the auditorium from the top seats. The stage is set up for marionettes, which will appear behind the curtain, and the caption unit is placed in the area just above the curtain, so that it can be seen comfortably from every seat. For rod productions, the caption unit is placed physically in the same area of the proscenium, but the captions appear below the stage action.

From a captioning perspective, two factors are to be taken into account. The first one is that the soundtrack is always recorded, an unusual practice in puppet theatre today, where the sound is normally delivered live. The use of recorded sound was more popular in the past, when the tradition of long-string marionettes, characterised by the puppeteers being out of view, was stronger. The absence of the puppeteers from the stage seemed to go hand in hand with the use of a recorded soundtrack, a practice that has been superseded by the introduction of live sound, which seems to respond better to the new trends in puppetry, and at the same time encourages the presence of the puppeteers on stage. Needless to say, the use of a recorded soundtrack facilitates the work of the captioner enormously. The captions can be timed to the soundtrack and launched automatically, similarly to how it is done at the cinema.

The second important characteristic that differentiates puppet theatre from actors' theatre is the lack of mouth movement. There are marionettes, and even more so rod puppets – for example, the famous Muppets by creators Jim and Jane Henson – that rely on mouth movement, but this is certainly not the rule in puppet theatre. From a captioning perspective, the lack of mouth movement gives more importance to speaker identification. Although there are theatrical conventions that dictate that the characters who are listening should not move, for the sake of immediacy and clarity, and because of the small scale of marionette theatre, speaker identification is a key element in captioning.

6.2.2 Puppet shows for younger children

In its repertoire, the Puppet Theatre Barge has two shows aimed at children aged three to eight years: *The Town Mouse and the Country Mouse* and the double bill *Captain Grimey* and *The Three Little Pigs*. These productions are the equivalent of pre-school children's programmes on broadcast media, characterised by slow-paced narrations and songs. While the placement of the captions below the stage is a choice dictated by logistics, linguistic and editing choices are guided by the age of the audiences these shows are aimed at. The main characteristics of these captions are:

- a maximum of two lines per caption
- edited dialogue
- the use of icons to identify speakers and to convey music and sound effects.

Since the pace of the speech is generally slow, the editing of dialogue is mainly constrained by the space allowed by a two-liner. Limiting the caption to a maximum of two lines ensures that an overload of text, which may discourage young children from engaging in reading, is avoided. With this in mind, syntactically complex sentences are sometimes simplified.

In an attempt to produce captions that may captivate young children, I decided to introduce icons to identify speakers, that is, pictures of the characters that are placed just before the lines are spoken, as shown in Figure 6.6 from *The Three Little Pigs and the Wolf*. This visual

Figure 6.6 Icons for speaker identification. Source: author

Figure 6.7 Icon for music. Source: author

equivalence between elements of the captions and the actions taking place on stage may ease the reading.

Similarly, instead of describing the music using text, I make use of icons that represent the instruments that are being played and the rhythm, as shown in Figure 6.7, which represents the music being played while the chase in *The Three Little Pigs and the Wolf* takes place.

As far as sound effects are concerned, they are often onomatopoeic in shows aimed at younger children: so if a car is beeping, an icon of the car appears, followed by the onomatopoeic 'beep, beep'.

When captioning for younger audiences, I have experimented with the use of images to indicate the source of the sound so as to make it more fun and appealing. Figure 6.8 shows an example from *The Three Little Pigs and the Wolf*.

In this particular case, the use of lower case for elements specific to d/Deaf and hard of hearing viewers was being explored during this stage production, as lower case is considered easier to read than upper case because of the greater exposure that readers have to it. As the viewers attending the show were young, I exploited all available techniques to facilitate the reading process.

These captions are somewhat different from the conventional captions with which audiences are acquainted and can therefore be defined as creative. However, I believe that creativity can be employed much more freely in the case of captioning for young audiences, as pre-school children are unlikely to be able to read full sentences, especially at a set speed. For this reason, it would be interesting to explore how the presence of isolated words that may be recognised

Figure 6.8 Icon for sound effect. Source: author

by shape and sight – and not necessarily according to reading ability – could complement the viewing experience in a didactic way. However, if older children or adults attend the puppet show, they may find that this type of creative captioning provides only limited access to the performance. Nothing prevents us from offering two or more types of captions for one and the same production to target the requirements of different age groups, but in this day and age, when not all theatre productions are made accessible to d/Deaf and hard of hearing audiences, such expectations are far too optimistic.

The captioning and subtitling software currently available does not allow for the inclusion of symbols or icons or for a more creative practice, so captioners have recourse to software that is not specifically designed for captioning, such as Apple Keynote or Microsoft PowerPoint. In work with these alternative programs, all the slides are normally given a black background and the captions are written in white (unless colours are used to identify speakers). Captioning with software that is not tailor-made is very time-consuming, as the text and icons need to be input into each slide individually and blank slides need to be inserted to account for spaces between the captions. The process of launching the captions live, however, is facilitated by the presentation view setting, which displays the upcoming caption as well as the current one.

Although the available software may be unsuitable, one of the rewards once the captions have been created is that a simple projector will allow the captioner to deliver a professional service to a d/Deaf and hard of hearing audience. An issue that may be encountered in captioning productions in which there are blackouts between scenes is that the beam of light from the projector may interfere with the theatre-makers' intention to achieve a total blackout, even if the projector is set to its lowest brightness setting. Often, these blackouts are required for scene changes that allow the puppeteers to transform the sets without being seen and to reveal a new setting in the space of a few seconds. One of the ways to hide the light beam is to use a moveable shutter, which can be manually operated. While this solution works well when there is no need for captions, the issue is present when relevant elements are to be captioned during the scene change. In situations like this one, a discussion between the captioner and the creative team may be enough to overcome the problem; for example, a black curtain could cover the scene for the duration of the blackout. This is another example of how collaboration between the creative team and the captioner during production can both benefit the captioned performance and preserve the quality of the play.

6.2.3 Puppet shows for older children

Most productions in the repertoire of the Puppet Theatre Barge are billed for everyone from three years of age; they range from adaptations of Aesop's fables, *Uncle Remus* by Joel Chandler Harris and *A Child's Garden of Verses* by Robert Louis Stevenson to an adaptation of Charles Dickens's *A Christmas Carol*. There are also marionette productions made with a child audience in mind. The captions are positioned above the stage, and the following parameters apply:

- flexibility in the number of lines (up to four)
- nearly verbatim transcription of dialogue exchanges
- use of colours or labels to identify speakers
- use of descriptive labels for music and sound effects.

The pace of the speech is generally slow, and so editing because of a high reading speed is seldom an issue. Although the captioner is aware of the amount of text present at once, the approach is more flexible than the one adopted for shows aimed at younger children, and, as mentioned, up to four lines can appear in a single caption. This may be to accommodate a full, long sentence with logical line-breaks or to fit a full music strophe – that is, a repeated group of lines of text which share a similar metre and rhyming scheme – in one caption.

Depending on the production, colours, or labels (e.g. [WOLF]), may be used to identify speakers. The introduction of lower case in labels was limited to the creative approach adopted for the captioning of productions aimed at older children and adults. Icons are not used for two reasons: older children and adults may be acquainted with conventional forms of speaker identification, and the subtitling software is not designed to allow for the insertion of icons. The choice between the two approaches – colours and labels – is often dictated by the show itself. If the characters have different predominant colours that can be easily matched to a legible caption colour, then identification may be implemented through the use of colours. This often needs a trial-and-error approach that requires testing. More often than not, labels are used because clear identification with colours is not easy. The insertion of labels to identify speakers requires space (a certain number of characters) and time to read them; however, information that is often repeated, such as the name of a character, may be recognised by shape, and may therefore require less reading time than the reading of new words. Figure 6.9 shows an example of speaker identification using labels from

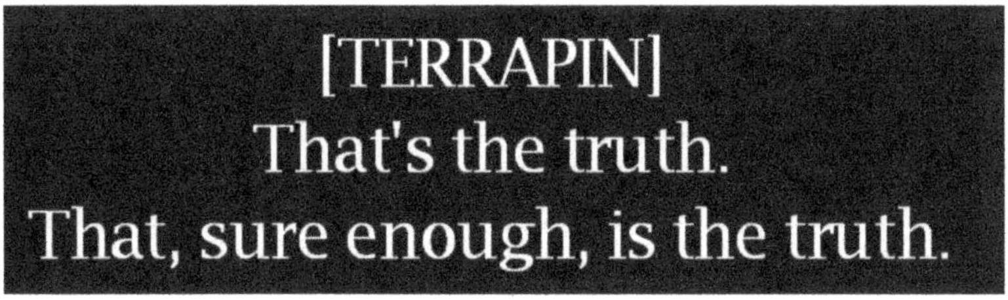

> [TERRAPIN]
> That's the truth.
> That, sure enough, is the truth.

Figure 6.9 Label for speaker identification. Source: author

Mr Rabbit Meets Brer Santa. Music, paralinguistic features and sound effects are also described verbally using labels, such as [MELODIC PIANO MUSIC], [LIVELY MUSIC], [OWL HOOTS] and [FOOTSTEPS]. If they happen off-screen, the typeface is by convention italicised.

The use of subtitling software – as opposed to Keynote – to caption productions aimed at older children makes the captioning process much quicker. On the day of the captioned performance, the captions are launched automatically as the audio and the captions are run through the same computer, using the subtitling software in replay mode. The potential issues with the projection of the captions are the same ones that can be encountered for productions aimed at younger children and discussed in section 6.2.2.

6.2.4 Puppet shows for adults

In the United Kingdom, people often associate puppetry with traditional Punch and Judy puppet shows, characterised by outrageous slapstick humour, which often includes violence. The belief that puppetry is aimed at young audiences is quite common, although less so in more recent years, which have witnessed the introduction of puppetry in mainstream theatre, perhaps encouraged by the success of *War Horse*, based on the novel by Michael Morpurgo, produced by Handspring Puppet Company and premiered in 2007 at the National Theatre. The Puppet Theatre Barge has been presenting drama for adults since 1982 and has approximately 20 adult productions in its repertoire. Some of the productions captioned since the service was launched in 2016 are *The Ancient Mariner* by Samuel Taylor Coleridge, *The Butterfly's Spell* by Federico García Lorca, *The River Girl* by Wendy Cope and *Spirit* by Susan Beattie.

Adult productions are captioned verbatim, that is word for word, in line with the approach adopted by Stagetext, the main provider of captions, as described in section 6.1.1. People can talk at up to 240 words per minute, with an average of 150 words per minute as a typical rate (Wald and Bain 2005). This data is relevant as it suggests that if we were subtitling verbatim, the reading speed could reach 240 words per minute. For media services providers like Netflix, editing of the source text is definitely not a priority, and reading speeds of 20 characters per second, that is, 240 words per minute – calculated on the assumption that an average English word contains five characters – are permitted (Netflix 2020a).

While reading speed is not a matter for debate in theatre captioning, possibly because Stagetext actively chooses the verbatim route, the extent to which words and expressions should be edited is one of the most discussed areas in subtitling for d/Deaf and hard of hearing audiences; many adults demand verbatim subtitles as a way of getting the same access to the programme as hearing audiences. It is interesting to note that within the field of subtitling for hearing audiences, it has always been accepted that, because of the spatio-temporal constraints imposed by the audiovisual medium, editing and reduction of the source text are inevitable. Besides these intrinsic, technical constraints, speech is absorbed quicker through hearing than through reading, and it must be remembered that the activity of reading subtitles is combined with that of watching images (Díaz-Cintas and Remael 2007). These reasons explain why subtitlers may opt for a reduction of the source text.

After a few years of captioning puppet shows, I have come to the conclusion that the editing of text needs to be reconsidered within the context of theatre. In my particular case, I am dealing with text based on poetry or stage adaptations of original plays, and so any form of textual editing is clearly to be discouraged. In my favour, the puppet shows that I caption have little in common with the fast-paced digital era we are exposed to in our daily lives and often the pace and speech rate are quite slow. In a way, the decision not to edit the text can be attributed to the intrinsic characteristics of the play.

However, on one occasion I worked on an unscripted play, *Spirit*, that contained a number of interviews with ordinary people about their other-worldly experiences. The dialogue exchanges were characterised by spontaneous speech, hesitations, repetitions, overlaps and inter-ruptions, and on some occasions they were incredibly fast-paced. I decided to keep as close to the original soundtrack as possible, sometimes reaching peak reading speeds of 250 words per minute. Occasionally, if the line contained several hesitations, I would edit some out to ease reading and would often use ellipsis as a way of helping the audience to match the caption to the audio as closely as possible. I focused my efforts on punctuation, segmentation and line-breaks to compensate for the rather ungrammatical subtitles that resulted from the verbatim approach. Besides following the school of thought of Stagetext, my decisions were guided by the understanding that the majority of d/Deaf and hard of hearing people have some access to sound. As a result, the captions may act as an aid to filling the gaps for them, a function that could not be fulfilled if the captions did not match the audio. This is also how Peter Pullan, one of the founders of Stagetext, justifies his preference for unedited verbatim captions (Stagetext 2019a).

The constraints of captioning puppet theatre differ from the ones imposed by the audiovisual medium. As an example, the captions for adult shows can contain up to six lines of text, as there is no risk of obscuring the images, which can clearly be an issue for films or television. While the captioner needs to be aware that a great amount of text presented at once can be overwhelming for young audiences, decisions on how to segment the text for adult productions can be guided by the onset and offset of speech, the poem's stanzas, and so on. Below is an example from *The Ancient Mariner*, the duration of the caption being 17 seconds and the reading speed 113 words per minute:

> With sloping masts and dipping prow,
> As who pursued with yell and blow
> Still treads the shadow of his foe,
> And forwards bends his head,
> The ship drove fast, loud roared the blast,
> And southward aye we fled.

The captioning of adult productions at the Puppet Theatre Barge follows quite a conventional approach and descriptive labels are used, always written in capital letters, to indicate elements specific to captioning for d/Deaf and hard of hearing audiences. To sum up, the parameters applied are as follows:

- flexibility in the number of lines (up to six)
- verbatim transcription of dialogue
- use of nominative or descriptive labels to identify speakers: [SYLVIA], [MARINER], [WITCHBEETLE]
- use of descriptive labels for music: [VIOLIN TUNING], [MELLOW VIBRAPHONE MELODY]

- use of descriptive labels for sound effects: [STRONG WHISTLING WIND], [EERIE OCEAN SOUNDS]
- use of descriptive labels for paralinguistic features: [CATERWAULING], [LAUGHTER AND HICCUPPING].

6.3 Marketing the captioned performance

Working in a captioned performance that is subsequently poorly attended by d/Deaf and hard of hearing people can be rather disheartening. In the first three years of captioning at the Puppet Theatre Barge, the turnout of d/Deaf and hard of hearing audiences has been rather low. I captioned 21 performances and they were attended by a total of 22 d/Deaf or hard of hearing patrons, that is, on average one person per show. As discussed in section 6.6, hearing members of the audience may also benefit from the captioned performances, and while this is encouraging, a great deal more needs to be done to reach our intended audience.

Having a good marketing strategy to reach the audiences is very important. The captioned performance should be advertised on the theatre's website, in all printed publicity, in social media and in all listings. Collaboration with other stakeholders is paramount; Stagetext publicises all captioned events, including ours, on its website (http://www.stagetext.org/whats-on).

For productions targeted at young audiences, I contact schools for deaf children, mainstream schools with provision for d/Deaf children and the National Deaf Children's Society (https://www.ndcs.org.uk). I connect either by direct contact or through social media.

For adult productions, I contact groups such as the National Association of Deafened People (http://www.nadp.org.uk), as well as others likely to include a significant number of people affected by deafness, such as Age UK (https://www.ageuk.org.uk).

Age being one of the main factors in deafness, the audiences for adult productions are more likely to include d/Deaf, deafened and hard of hearing people than those for children. Often, older people arrive at the theatre without knowing that the performance is actually being captioned, or that there is an induction loop they can connect to.

As tickets are usually bought beforehand and online, they should state that the performance is captioned, and the projection of a first caption before the show starts should also provide this information. It is important to let the audience know about the presence of the induction loop, which can be done through the use of induction-loop system signs positioned in several places in the venue.

Although the ultimate aim of a captioner, who has worked hard to make the performance accessible, is to welcome a high number of d/Deaf and hard of hearing people to the show, when the audience is only or predominantly hearing, the captioner should also be motivated to enable inclusiveness within the theatre.

6.4 Before the captioned performance

Besides the creation of the captions and the marketing of the captioned performance, there are some final preparations to be made before the big day. I try to have the captions ready before the end of the rehearsals period. This way I can have them proofread by one of the directors of the Puppet Theatre Barge and do a trial while the puppeteers are still rehearsing; this will often be at a dress rehearsal. The trial, besides being a rehearsal for the captioner, is useful for highlighting any technical issues that may occur; for example, the visibility of the captions could be affected by the lighting, or the captions may interfere with some special effects. At this time, the captioner and the creative team can have conversations to overcome challenges.

It is important to test the equipment, particularly laptops, projectors and the induction loop, a few days before the captioned show in order to have time to solve any last-minute issues. Lastly, feedback questionnaires are prepared and printed to be ready for the audiences on the day.

6.5 On the day of the captioned performance

The captioner arrives at the venue approximately two hours before the doors open to the public. This time is devoted to checking that the equipment is in working order. Occasionally, the captioner may need to set up an extra projector; this happened during one of the productions at the Puppet Theatre Barge, *Spirit*, which used projections as well as live puppetry. In cases like this, the main projector, normally set up for the captions, is used to project films (duly subtitled); another projector and a laptop are used for the narration voiced over the puppetry scenes, which are cued live.

The captioner may have to liaise with the front-of-house person and the puppeteers to answer any questions they may have related to the captioned show. At the Puppet Theatre Barge, audiences collect their paper tickets on arrival. The front-of-house person will make sure that the tickets indicate that the performance is captioned. This information is given, before the performance, on the website, in all the publicity and at the time of booking.

At the Puppet Theatre Barge, which has an audience capacity of 50, the caption unit is visible from all the seats and the induction loop encloses all the seats in the auditorium, so d/Deaf and hard of hearing audiences do not need to be allocated specific seats. This is a positive aspect in the sense that our audience do not need to make any specific arrangements for their visit.

While the public take their seats, and up until the very start of the show, a caption is displayed announcing the captioned performance and also stating that captioning gives access to the play to d/Deaf, deafened and hard of hearing people (Figure 6.10). The captioner hands out feedback questionnaires – reproduced in Appendix 1 – aimed at collecting the patrons' views on the captioned performance and to be completed after the show.

If the captions are being launched live, the back row of the auditorium is reserved for the captioner. In cases where the delivery of the captions is done automatically, the captioner will still be present at the performance. Occasionally, when the captioner is engaged to work as a puppeteer for a season and is performing on the day of the captioned performance, she will ask a colleague to watch from the front while the laptop is kept backstage to check that the delivery of the captions is running smoothly.

The captioner should avoid sitting at the front of the auditorium, as the brightness from the laptop can be distracting for the audience, unless a captioning booth is made available. All the same, the captioner sat in the front row for the performance of *Spirit*, because the projector needed to be manually operated through the use of a moveable shutter that would block out the projector light beam in the absence of captions.

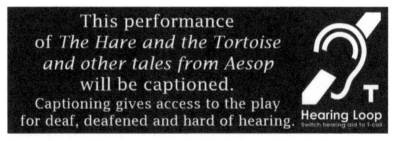

Figure 6.10 Caption announcing the captioned performance. Source: author

The completed feedback questionnaires are collected and a record is kept so as to monitor any issues that may come up. At the end of the performance, one last caption invites the audience, as an alternative or in addition to the feedback questionnaires on paper, to express their views by email, and lets them know about the next captioned performance on the schedule. The captioner stays around after the show in case members of the audience want to talk about the captions, as it is important that the audience feel they have a point of contact.

6.6 Audience's feedback on captioned puppet shows

The feedback provided by the audience is extremely important, as it helps the captioner to monitor attendance by d/Deaf and hard of hearing people and to identify and address potential issues, mainly of a technical nature. It is also informative about how audiences perceive the captions. The questionnaire includes two open-ended questions – one examining more specific features, such as the presentation of dialogue, music and sound effects – and the other more generally inviting audiences to express their thoughts and views on any other aspects of the captioned performance.

In the first three years since the launch of the captioning service in October 2016, 14 novel productions were captioned. The captioner's commitment to d/Deaf and hard of hearing audiences is to offer at least one captioned performance per season. The duration of a season varies between two weeks and three months. Since some productions had more than one season, the total number of captioned performances in the three years was 21. Table 6.1 lists them and groups them according to their target audience.

6.6.1 Audience demographics

Over the years, I have collected a total of 209 questionnaires, an average of 10 respondents per performance, of which one member of the audience, per show, was d/Deaf or hard of hearing. To be more specific, 11 were d/Deaf and 11 were hard of hearing.

It is quite unusual for audiences to be exposed to a captioned puppet show. In fact, I am not aware of any other puppet shows being captioned anywhere in the world. The set-up of the captions for marionette productions at the Puppet Theatre Barge is a small version of what happens at the opera. In fact, many hearing respondents seemed to associate the caption performances with the surtitles that can be

Table 6.1   Captioned puppet shows and their target audience

Audience	Productions
Adults	*The Ancient Mariner* by Samuel Taylor Coleridge
	The Butterfly's Spell by Federico García Lorca
	The River Girl by Wendy Cope
	Spirit by Susan Beattie
Older children	*Monkey Business*
	A Child's Garden of Verses by Robert Louis Stevenson
	Joey's Circus Comes to Town by Glyn Edwards
	The Little Christmas Tree
	Mr Rabbit Meets Brer Santa
	A Christmas Carol by Charles Dickens
	Red Riding Hood by Deborah Jones
Younger children	*Captain Grimey* and *The Three Little Pigs*
	The Town Mouse and the Country Mouse

enjoyed at the opera. One third of respondents confirmed that they had been exposed to captions or surtitles before the captioned puppet show.

6.6.2 Visibility of the caption unit

The auditorium of the Puppet Theatre Barge, as described in section 6.2.1, is quite small: it has only a 50-seat capacity. This favours the visibility of the caption unit, which is placed above the stage area for marionette productions and below the stage area for rod productions. The vast majority of the respondents, 97 per cent, had no problem being able to see the caption unit. However, some visibility issues came up, which are ultimately intrinsic to the set-up used. The theatre is not equipped with an LED screen, which is what Stagetext uses as a caption unit. An ordinary overheard projector is used. This means that the opening of the projector lens needs to be adjusted so that the light of the beam does not spill into parts of the proscenium that are not intended to be lit. The edges of the lens are covered, which makes the edges of the projection become blurred. This has very rarely been noticed by audiences, and only 2 per cent of the respondents mentioned it. It is a logistics issue that, in the long term, requires a change in the equipment used. In the meantime, the issue is overcome by using the maximum number of lines and the maximum number of characters per line only if absolutely necessary, so as to avoid having any part of the text placed too close to the edges. I may, for example, insert a line-break, or segment the text differently, in order to create a margin of distance between the text and the edges of the beam of light.

6.6.3 Did captions improve access to or enjoyment of the play?

Particularly revealing were the answers to the question 'Did captions improve access to or enjoyment of the play?', to which 79 per cent of respondents answered positively, as shown in Figure 6.11. All d/Deaf and hard of hearing people, 22 per cent of the sample, are of course part of the 'yes' cohort; they added comments such as: 'No question that without captions I would not have understood anything so the captions give me 100 per cent access' (deaf person who watched the double bill *Captain Grimey* and *The Three Little Pigs* on 20 July 2019).

Most interestingly, contrary to common belief, only a minority of hearing people – 6 per cent – answered the question negatively, which is a very small group of hearing people who feel strongly opposed to

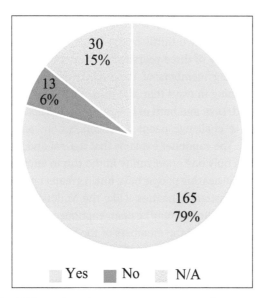

Figure 6.11 Did captions improve access to or enjoyment of the play?. Source: author

captions. Some of the comments show that captions can cause some frustration, such as: 'We didn't choose a performance with captions. It was the only one with seats available. Perhaps you should ask people when they book whether they require captions. If not, they could be omitted' (hearing person who watched *The Butterfly's Spell* on 22 September 2018). Another, similar view was: 'It distracted from the stage/puppetry. Should be reserved for special performances. No one here seemed hard of hearing tonight' (hearing person who watched *The Butterfly's Spell* on 22 September 2018). Comments of this nature are very rare. However, such views suggest that part of the role of the captioner is to sensitise audiences to the value of captioning for d/Deaf and hard of hearing people and about why inclusiveness is important. As already mentioned, at the Puppet Theatre Barge there is one open-captioned performance per run. It can be attended by anyone, without the need to make any specific arrangements. It is important to make sure that the captioned performance is advertised as such and that people booking to attend are made aware that they are booking for a captioned performance. On arrival, audiences are reminded that the performance will be captioned; this is written on their tickets and there are signs announcing it. When the audience take their seats, they will see a caption that announces that the performance will be captioned and explains what captioning is. The questionnaires are normally handed out just after people have taken their seats and have had a chance to look around. The captioner often engages in conversation with members of the audience who have never attended a captioned performance – at least two-thirds of the total – and may ask questions about it. In the course of three years, only two unpleasant incidents took place, when hearing members of the audience questioned the whole concept of captioning in ways that showed complete unawareness of the requirements of d/Deaf and hard of hearing people. Those incidents offer an opportunity to challenge people's misconceptions and advocate for open captioning. The captioner explains that d/Deaf and hard of hearing patrons are given only one opportunity in the run to attend an accessible performance, while hearing people have much greater choice. And it is not so different in mainstream theatres – like the National Theatre – where two performances in the run may be open-captioned.

About 15 per cent of the members of the audience neither engaged with the captions – some said they 'tried to ignore' them or were 'indifferent' – nor recognised that the captions might be valuable to other people attending the show.

Going back to the 'yes' cohort, 57 per cent of the hearing audience either actively recognised that the captions are a valuable tool for d/Deaf and hard of hearing viewers and supported their provision, or said that the captions enhanced their own enjoyment of the play, or both. Twelve respondents – 6 per cent of the entire group – pointed out that the captions are useful for non-native speakers of English; a member of the audience who attended *The Butterfly's Spell* on 20 January 2019 explained: 'I'm not a native speaker [of English] so it was good to have subtitles that gave more understanding of Lorca's text.'

There were instances of hearing people commenting that the captions were an asset to the production. The following are statements reported by attendees of *Spirit* on 17 November 2019: 'It was a wonderful visual addition to the show' and 'They [the captions] illustrated the narrative in a beautiful way.'

Poetry and captions seem to complement each other, as suggested by an attendee of *The River Girl* on 17 November 2017: 'It was nice to have the addition of the written poems. Made the show even better!' Attendees of *The Butterfly's Spell* on 22 September 2018 made these comments:

'Nice to be able to read the beautiful poetry as well as hearing it.'

'Sometimes we found the words of the poem so beautiful, it was a treat to also be able to read them.'

'Because the play was based on a poem, it was great to have the captions to get an idea of how it was written.'

Some productions aimed at younger children, such as *The Town Mouse and the Country Mouse*, contain quite a few well-known traditional songs. During the captioned performances, audiences are generally more vocal and enjoy singing along, as confirmed by a member of the audience who attended the performance of 23 March 2019: 'We could sing along.' Children may also enjoy reading along, as suggested by comments such as 'The captions kept children occupied' (attendee of *The Hare and the Tortoise and other tales from Aesop* on 18 June 2017) and 'My six year old granddaughter enjoyed reading along with it' (attendee of *Captain Grimey* and *The Three Little Pigs* on 20 July 2019).

The captioner experimented with the use of creative captioning in an attempt to render the captions less text-based and more accessible and appealing to young audiences, as discussed in section 6.2.2. This aspect was very much a topic of conversation in the open-ended questions, as shown below, in the feedback received from two deaf senior members of the audience who attended *Captain Grimey* and *The Three Little Pigs* on 20 July 2019:

> 'I like the use of drawings of characters to indicate speaker and use of musical instruments to illustrate music playing (orchestral). Sound effects, e.g. clock, charming but important function in enabling me to hear.'

> 'Wonderful idea to indicate who was speaking by putting picture of speaker on caption line.'

For me, the questionnaires served as an informative tool to improve my practice. A summary of the feedback received is available in Appendix 2.

6.7 Subtitling live events

In addition to theatre plays, there are other live events than can be made accessible to d/Deaf and hard of hearing visitors. Museums and galleries, for example, are places that in principle would appear to be inclusive, as the experience is mainly visual and the exhibits are often accompanied by labels. For those who have sign language as their preferred method of communication, well-known museums and galleries generally offer tours and talks in sign language led by d/Deaf presenters. These are, however, one-off events, similarly to open-caption performances in theatres.

The provision of induction loops in public spaces benefits hearing aid and cochlear implant users. Some entertainment venues may offer an infrared system as an alternative. This latter option requires the collection of a receiver from the venue; it will have a neck loop, if the visitor has a hearing aid, or, alternatively, headphones. Other facilities may include audio guides with volume enhancement or transcripts of audio guides.

A deeper engagement with the exhibition can be provided for a wider range of d/Deaf and hard of hearing visitors not only by subtitling any audiovisual material present in the exhibition, but also by offering live subtitling for the talks and lectures scheduled as part of the venue's cultural programme. Other contexts in which live subtitling proves to be particularly useful are conferences, festivals, and post-show talks in the theatre and other venues.

Guided tours can be subtitled live by a stenographer and delivered to the user as a closed solution. The stenographer listens to the speaker on a mobile phone on loudspeaker and sends a verbatim transcription to a web browser, which is delivered as text to a handheld device.

Another way of delivering live subtitling is through respeaking. While, in the case of broadcast television, the use of stenography in Europe has been superseded by respeaking, at live events the latter is not quite as established.

The skills required by speech-to-text reporters and respeakers are very different, as discussed in section 1.4.1. Logistically the respeaker of live events has an added challenge when working onsite, as a set-up similar to that of a conference interpreter's booth would be required. An alternative is respeaking into a special mask that softens the voice. Respeakers can also work remotely.

6.8 Discussion points

6.8.1   Find out what theatre captioning solutions, if any, are available in your country and assess the number of captioned performances monthly available in your town or city.

6.8.2   Choose a clip from https://www.youtube.com/c/National TheatreOnline/videos and make a list of the challenges the play presents for a captioner, both linguistically and logistically. For example, where should the caption unit be positioned? Would conversations with the stage manager or theatre staff help you to overcome those challenges?

6.8.3   Imagine you are approached by an independent small theatre willing to launch a captioning service and asked for advice on how to get started. Visit accessibletheatre.org.uk/access-co-ordinators/captioning for informed practice on captioning theatre performances and make an initial plan of the required steps and advice to be given to your client.

Note

1   The Epson smart glasses were first introduced at the Avignon Festival, France, in 2015, by Panthea, providers of surtitling solutions for the performing arts.

Appendix 1
Questionnaire collected after a captioned performance

Spirit

Captioned performance at the Puppet Theatre Barge
on 7 September 2019

1. Specify if you are:

   a. Hearing
   b. Hard of Hearing
   c. Deaf

2. Have you attended any other captioned performances in the past?
   If so, please mention play and/or theatre.

3. Could you see the caption unit clearly?

4. Did captions improve access to or enjoyment of the play?

5. What comments or suggestions do you have on the captions
   (of dialogues, music and sound effects)?

6. Do you have any other comments?

7. Would you like to be notified of future captioned performances?
   If so, please provide us with your email address.

Thank you for your feedback!

Appendix 2
Summary of feedback from captioned puppet shows

		The Hare and the Tortoise and Other Tales from Aesop	Captain Grimey and The Three Little Pigs
		18 June 2017	6 August 2017
Specify if you are:	a. Hearing	11	6
	b. Hard of hearing	0	0
	c. Deaf	2	0
Have you attended any other captioned performances in the past?	yes	5	0
	no	8	6
Could you see the caption unit clearly?	yes	12	6
	no	1	0
Did captions improve access to or enjoyment of the play?	yes	10	6
	no	1	0
	NA	2	0

(continued)

(continued)

	The Hare and the Tortoise and Other Tales from Aesop	Captain Grimey and The Three Little Pigs
	18 June 2017	6 August 2017
What comments or suggestions do you have on the captions (of dialogues, music and sound effects)?	I enjoyed the innovation of having extra clues (instruments and animals). (DEAF)	It was enjoyable as it was synchronised.
	I loved the way the sound effects were shown.	They are good.
	Loved the icons.	Enjoyed the captions very much.
	Dialogues were perhaps a bit too long. Laughter was not captioned. Loved the emojis with animals and music.	Well done.
	I liked the icons.	
Do you have any other comments?	Very clear, readable and enjoyable.	Great for me as a non-native speaker.
	I think the captions provide maximum accessibility to deaf and HoH people. Very clear.	
	All very well done.	
	The captions kept children occupied.	
	The captions improved access, specially [as] the language is not my first language. Not sure if the 4 or 5 line subtitles work for SDH users.	
	Need to have brighter white. (DEAF)	

		The Hare and the Tortoise and Other Tales from Aesop	The River Girl
		22 August 2017	8 September 2017
Specify if you are:	a. Hearing	7	11
	b. Hard of hearing	0	0
	c. Deaf	0	1
Have you attended any other captioned performances in the past?	yes	1	7
	no	6	5
Could you see the caption unit clearly?	yes	7	12
	no	0	0
Did captions improve access to or enjoyment of the play?	yes	4	10
	no	1	0
	NA	2	2
What comments or suggestions do you have on the captions (of dialogues, music and sound effects)?		Very clear.	I thought it was all fantastic.
		I didn't like the pictures, they were too big.	Captions are fine.
			They were clear, witty and generally enjoyable.
			Very clear dialogue, watch for spelling mistakes.
			Well put together. I wonder if there could be more info about what music is playing or perhaps this could be handed out before/after the show.

(continued)

(continued)

Do you have any other comments?	The Hare and the Tortoise and Other Tales from Aesop	The River Girl
	22 August 2017	8 September 2017
	Very well presented.	Can be distracting but also quite nice to see the words.
	During the storm, the screen of the subtitles was visible on the rain drop.	Captions might be useful for deaf people.
	I wasn't reading them, I was watching the puppets (Q4). They were fine. Sometimes the voiceover and the captions were different.	It helped me understand the story better. Interesting to see if it would improve with interpreter as much as captions. Would be interesting to see if 'easy read' captions would be easier to understand than full English captions for the Deaf / BSL. (DEAF)
	Good for those that need them	It was very helpful to have the text.
		It's useful for non-native speakers.
		I am very impressed.
		Excellent as there was enough time to read the captions but also enjoy the show. My worry was that you would only read the captions not enjoying the show but this did not happen.

		Captain Grimey and *The Three Little Pigs*	*The River Girl*
		23 October 2017	17 November 2017
Specify if you are:	a. Hearing	5	8
	b. Hard of hearing	0	1
	c. Deaf	0	1
Have you attended any other captioned performances in the past?	yes	1	2
	no	4	8
Could you see the caption unit clearly?	yes	4	8
	no	1	0
Did captions improve access to or enjoyment of the play?	yes	3	6
	no	1	1
	NA	1	3
What comments or suggestions do you have on the captions (of dialogues, music and sound effects)?		Music was good plus sound effects.	All great! They were great in terms of describing the mood of the music. Very good. Adequate.

(continued)

(continued)

	Captain Grimey and The Three Little Pigs	The River Girl
	23 October 2017	17 November 2017
Do you have any other comments?	All looked great	I found the captions distracting. I had to focus on the show to get the usual personal effect. I would not come to the captioned performance again, but it is a good effort, and I am sure if I was deaf it would be great. Well done being inclusive!
	3- to 8-year-old may not be able to read.	I tried to ignore the captions.
	Excellent.	The font was fitting and captions not too bright.
	Brilliant set-up.	I don't need the captions but I didn't think they were invasive to someone with full hearing. I have friends with hearing issues and so think it is great that this is accessible to all.
		The captions were not at all obstructive/distracting. It was nice to have the addition of the written poems. Made the show even better!

	Excellent initiative.
	The captions enhanced my enjoyment.
	Improved understanding because English is not my first language.
	I found the words easier to follow. Didn't find it distracting, just helpful.

(continued)

		The Little Christmas Tree 23 December 2017	Joey's Circus Comes to Town 23 January 2018
Specify if you are:	a. Hearing	7	6
	b. Hard of hearing	0	1
	c. Deaf	2	0
Have you attended any other captioned performances in the past?	yes	2	1
	no	7	6
Could you see the caption unit clearly?	yes	9	7
	no	0	0
Did captions improve access to or enjoyment of the play?	yes	7	6
	no	0	0
	NA	2	1
What comments or suggestions do you have on the captions (of dialogues, music and sound effects)?		The sounds and effects are fascinating. Excellent. All good It seemed very well done. Lovely music. (DEAF)	
Do you have any other comments?		Indifferent. Captions did not make much difference.	Well done, it helped if you couldn't hear. (HOH)

The captions disappeared as the performance was too absorbing.	Everything's been very clear, even not just for people who have difficulties hearing. It's useful for people who don't feel confident with English.
Useful to have the loop too.	Captions helped clarify some of the characters' speech.
	It's great they could improve access for others. I guess you could widen your audience and change language, e.g. do French performances.
	The edges weren't as visible. Captions didn't detract from enjoyment of play.

		Monkey Business 7 April 2018	Red Riding Hood 9 June 2018
Specify if you are:	a. Hearing	8	7
	b. Hard of hearing	0	1
	c. Deaf	0	0
Have you attended any other captioned performances in the past?	yes	2	2
	no	6	6
Could you see the caption unit clearly?	yes	8	8
	no	0	0
Did captions improve access to or enjoyment of the play?	yes	4	6
	no	2	0
	NA	2	2
What comments or suggestions do you have on the captions (of dialogues, music and sound effects)?		Great.	Sometimes it wasn't clear which captions were for the background sounds and which weren't.
		It was great and easily visible.	Bottom line a little difficult to read at the beginning. Otherwise very clear.
		Good idea.	
		All brilliant.	

Do you have any other comments?		
	Didn't improve access for me but great to have.	Sitting near the back it was perfect. You wouldn't want it to be brighter. I did not need the access, but it wasn't distracting. It helped since Granny's voice is a little bit indistinct.
	Though we didn't need the captions, it's nice to offer and didn't distract us.	The red [magenta] captions were somewhat dark and difficult to read. A brighter shade of red would be better.
	Great for the hard of hearing.	All really good.
		Absolutely improved because English is not my first language.

		The Town Mouse and the Country Mouse	The Butterfly's Spell
		21 July 2018	22 September 2018
Specify if you are:	a. Hearing	7	18
	b. Hard of hearing	1	0
	c. Deaf	0	0
Have you attended any other captioned performances in the past?	yes	4	3
	no	4	15
Could you see the caption unit clearly?	yes	8	18
	no	0	0
Did captions improve access to or enjoyment of the play?	yes	6	15
	no	0	2
	NA	2	1
What comments or suggestions do you have on the captions (of dialogues, music and sound effects)?		I liked the musical note.	Perhaps miss out the initial 'haunting music' caption as it caused laughs, which wasn't very atmospheric!
		Perfect.	Too bright, especially when the stage depicts night time.
		Easy to read. (HOH)	The accuracy of the captions in text and timing was impressive and very greatly improved their use.
		Good	The music note was very helpful to point out the songs.

	They were perfect!	I liked the description of the music, the names and accents of the characters. Also, nice to be able to read the beautiful poetry as well as hearing it.
		The music was incredible. The butterfly's song in particular was very affecting and went so well with the lyrics.
		Definitely improved one's hearing of dialogues.
		I thought they were perfect.
		Wasn't sure about the music descriptions.
		Because the play was based on a poem, it was great to have the captions to get an idea of how it was written.
Do you have any other comments?	Greatly appreciated. (HOH)	We didn't choose a performance with captions. It was the only one with seats available. Perhaps you should ask people when they book whether they require captions. If not, they could be omitted.

(continued)

(continued)

The Town Mouse and the Country Mouse	The Butterfly's Spell
21 July 2018	22 September 2018
	They [somewhat] detracted from the performance of the marionettes. More of the puppets, less of the poetry, music and captions.
	As a hearing person the captions, being large in relation to the small stage, detracted a little from the audible dialogue. Make it smaller?
	It distracted from the stage/puppetry. Should be reserved for special performances. No one here seemed hard of hearing tonight.
	For me the captions helped a lot with the English because I am foreigner.
	The captions improved access as they made it much easier to follow given English is not my first language.
	They improved access because English is my second language.

All appropriate and useful (captions are distracting if one can hear but this was easily outweighed by the usefulness/extra information).	
Sometimes we found the words of the poem so beautiful, it was a treat to also be able to read them.	
Great, beautiful verse captured beautifully in the captions.	
The captions can help follow the line of thought, especially when it is as poetic as Garcia Lorca's.	
Because the speed of light (captions) is so much greater than the speed of sound, one can hear very clearly.	

		The Town Mouse and the Country Mouse 27 October 2018	Mr Rabbit Meets Brer Santa 1 December 2018
Specify if you are:	a. Hearing	7	12
	b. Hard of hearing	1	0
	c. Deaf	0	0
Have you attended any other captioned performances in the past?	yes	2	3
	no	6	9
Could you see the caption unit clearly?	yes	7	12
	no	0	0
Did captions improve access to or enjoyment of the play?	yes	7	9
	no	0	0
	NA	1	3
What comments or suggestions do you have on the captions (of dialogues, music and sound effects)?		Liked the picture to indicate who's talking. Slightly smaller.	I liked it very much. Perhaps add instrument. Moonlight Sonata was correct of course but it was a special one with saxophone. Speaking too quickly.

Do you have any other comments?	Wasn't too disturbing, just right. It helped to understand what the puppets were saying.	Well done, doesn't get in the way.
	There are some mistakes but really good and easy to follow.	Even for a hearing person, it was sometimes hard to hear, so captions helped a great deal!
	Music a bit louder. (HOH)	Love them.
	Not necessary for me but good idea.	Very clear and understandable
		They were non-intrusive in my case.

		The Butterfly's Spell 20 January 2019	The Town Mouse and the Country Mouse 23 March 2019
Specify if you are:	a. Hearing	12	12
	b. Hard of hearing	0	0
	c. Deaf	0	0
Have you attended any other captioned performances in the past?	yes	6	11
	no	6	0
Could you see the caption unit clearly?	yes	12	12
	no	0	0
Did captions improve access to or enjoyment of the play?	yes	11	9
	no	0	2
	NA	1	1
What comments or suggestions do you have on the captions (of dialogues, music and sound effects)?		The sound effects were easily understood. The music captions were adequate. I liked how there was a music note next to the captions when someone was singing.	Great to have captions for music. All good. I think they were well devised. For the sound of the car approaching there could be captions (not only beep beep).
Do you have any other comments?		Perhaps make it clear on the website that captioned performances are open to everyone. Great that you do them.	As I have very good hearing, I didn't need them and found them a slight distraction but I'm sure they are useful for people who are hard of hearing.
		Useful to improve understanding.	I was a bit distracted by the captions.

The edges of the text could be a bit clearer. The captions are quite useful (even if you're not deaf!)	The captions were very good. We think that captioned performances could be useful for foreigners too.
I enjoyed being able to read the text. Was it relevant to mention accent? Not sure, is this the case?	We could sing along.
The captions help to get the background story clear. If you want the captions suitable for second speakers too, shorter sentences in the beginning would be better, probably. But it's a great opportunity for foreign visitors to follow the poetic, unusual words.	I think it was better with captions.
The captions improve access, specially if you are not English speaker.	Why not have all performances captioned?
I'm not a native speaker so it was good to have subtitles that gave more understanding of Lorca's text.	Faded in and out, so not too jolting. Slide in or add small character.
The captions were easy to understand.	
The captions were useful to check my understanding of some words. They also sometimes took away from the magical aspect. Very good idea. Could they be higher up away from stage? Very important to have.	
The captions give more information but take out attention from the dolls' details.	

		A Child's Garden of Verses	Spirit
		29 June 2019	7 September 2019
Specify if you are:	a. Hearing	5	12
	b. Hard of hearing	1	3
	c. Deaf	0	1
Have you attended any other captioned performances in the past?	yes	1	6
	no	5	10
Could you see the caption unit clearly?	yes	5	15
	no	0	1
Did captions improve access to or enjoyment of the play?	yes	6	14
	no	0	1
	NA	0	1
What comments or suggestions do you have on the captions (of dialogues, music and sound effects)?		All good. (HOH) Good.	Maybe the music could be better described. Maybe more background into style of music. (DEAF) Perfect. All good. Fitted perfectly. Great music. Described well, good interpretation of music and speech.

		Sometimes during the moaning agitated woman's song I might have chosen different words, e.g. 'non-verbal' instead of 'unintelligible' and then 'high-pitched cries' firstly sounded more curious or joyous whereas later cries sounded more anguished, but this is all subjective. Overall I thought the font, word and everything used all suited the atmosphere and complemented the essence of the show.
		Words to dialogue were fine. I wondered if there were words missing to some of music but I could be wrong. Sound effects, very good.
		All very clear and sensitive to the performance.
Do you have any other comments?	Great for every show.	The person operating the computer at the front needed a bigger shawl as I saw the bright screen frequently.

(continued)

(continued)

A Child's Garden of Verses	Spirit
29 June 2019	7 September 2019
It absolutely improves enjoyment of the play. I specially love when the caption allows me to notice the wordplay sponge-taneous. When the background is a bit too bright, the bottom caption, particularly the non-white colours, are a bit hard to read.	Without captions would not understand anything. I look forward to another captioned performance. (HOH)
	Excellent work. Only frustration your laptop was too bright at front, need to cover better. (DEAF)
	Captions helped when I couldn't understand the cockney (and I have perfect hearing).
	It was interesting to see the show in captions as well as hear it. It made me think about having captions in other languages as well.
	Louder music or more bass. I could feel the more upbeat songs a bit in my feet. If you adjusted the bass level and turned up the overall volume it might help more people with limited hearing 'feel' and engage with the music.

	Occasionally captions helped when things were harder to hear but otherwise weren't in the way.
	The operation of the captions meant some of the stage was obscured.
	I couldn't see all the captions because I was sitting at the very back and I'm a little short-sighted. Larger letters for the captions? The captions are very useful even for people who hear well in the case of accents or when the actors/the dialogues are not clear.

		Spirit	*Captain Grimey and The Three Little Pigs*
		17 November 2019	20 July 2019
Specify if you are:	a. Hearing	11	5
	b. Hard of hearing	2	0
	c. Deaf	1	2
Have you attended any other captioned performances in the past?	yes	4	3
	no	11	4
Could you see the caption unit clearly?	yes	14	7
	no	0	0
Did the captions improve access and/or enjoyment of the play?	yes	12	7
	no	2	0
	NA	0	0
What comments or suggestions do you have on the captions (of dialogues, music and sound effects)?		I just wonder if there is a way of invoking the music more?	I like the use of drawings of characters to indicate speaker and use of musical instruments to illustrate music playing (orchestral). Sound effects e.g. clock charming but important function in enabling me to hear. (DEAF)
		Beautiful.	Wonderful idea to indicate who was speaking by putting picture of speaker on caption line. (DEAF)

	Very good.
	All worked really well. My 6-year-old granddaughter enjoyed reading along with it.
	I liked the placement and the font and the character icon.
	When the stage was yellow light, the letters were not bright enough. Captions should have been brighter.
Do you have any other comments?	Too close in proximity to the visual space. Greater spacing above the stage would be less intrusive. Very good and inclusive.
	No question that without captions I would not have understood anything so the captions give me 100% access. Not always sure that editing needed. (DEAF)
	Even though I don't need to I always used subs because it helps me concentrate more. Everything should have subs.
	Loop works wonderfully. Captioning easy to read and wonderfully timed. Need more deaf people.
	It was a wonderful visual addition to the show.
	The light from the beam of the projector added to it.
	All very accurate.
	They illustrated the narrative in a beautiful way.
	Even though not deaf, it was well placed and easy to see without being intrusive.
	The captions changed quite quickly.

		Captain Grimey and The Three Little Pigs 7 December 2019	**Total**
Specify if you are:	a. Hearing	10	187
	b. Hard of hearing	0	11
	c. Deaf	1	11
Have you attended any other captioned performances in the past?	yes	4	70
	no	7	139
Could you see the caption unit clearly?	yes	11	202
	no	0	3
Did captions improve access to or enjoyment of the play?	yes	7	165
	no	0	13
	NA	3	30
What comments or suggestions do you have on the captions (of dialogues, music and sound effects)?		Generally quite good (occasional lag, but minor). I liked the clarifying images. Perhaps a little more clarity on the picture of the character who is being captioned. Maybe could be slightly bigger/clearer.	

Do you have any other comments?	
	This is a really good idea for people who could not hear and also for foreign people it is easier to understand the performance.
	They were easy to read even from the back.
	This is very, very good, beautiful comic timing. (DEAF)
	Looked wonderful.
	Excellent simplification of captions.

Appendix 3
Example of subtitles for clip from *School of Rock*

0001 00:00:00:00 00:00:02:17 **OK? There used to be a way to stick it to the Man.**	0010 00:00:29:14 00:00:32:22 **On Tuesdays, the children have music class now.**
0002 00:00:02:19 00:00:04:08 **It was called rock 'n' roll.**	0011 00:00:32:24 00:00:35:12 **Right, OK. Ah, good work, people.**
0003 00:00:05:00 00:00:06:18 **But guess what. Oh, no!**	0012 00:00:35:14 00:00:39:09 **We will continue with our lecture on the Man when we return.**
0004 00:00:06:24 00:00:10:02 **The Man ruined that too with a little thing called MTV!**	0013 00:00:39:24 00:00:41:11 **Have a good music class.**
0005 00:00:11:01 00:00:15:09 **So, don't waste your time trying to make anything cool, pure or awesome**	0014 00:00:48:19 00:00:55:01 **[INSTRUMENTS PLAY CLASSICAL MUSIC]**
0006 00:00:15:11 00:00:19:04 **'cause the Man's just gonna call you a fat loser and crush your soul.**	0015 00:01:00:10 00:01:04:08 **[INSTRUMENTS CONTINUE PLAYING]**
0007 00:00:19:06 00:00:21:16 **So, do yourselves a favour and just give up!**	0016 00:01:52:22 00:01:58:22 *[ROCK MUSIC: "SUNSHINE OF YOUR LOVE" BY CREAM]*
0008 00:00:25:05 00:00:26:17 **Oh!**	0017 00:02:11:04 00:02:13:13 **[GUITAR STRUM]**
0009 00:00:27:06 00:00:29:00 **Mr Schneebly, it's after 10.**	0018 00:02:16:04 00:02:17:23 **Mr S, what's going on?**

0019 00:02:20:09 00:02:24:18 I heard you in music class. You, guys, can really play.	0034 00:03:33:16 00:03:35:03 Yes!
0020 00:02:25:04 00:02:27:04 [SHOUTS] Why didn't anyone tell me?	0035 00:03:37:09 00:03:39:14 OK, you stay right there. Don't move.
0021 00:02:27:06 00:02:29:14 - You. What's your name? - Zack.	0036 00:03:39:23 00:03:41:18 Piano man, front and centre.
0022 00:02:29:24 00:02:31:14 - You play the guitar? - Yeah.	0037 00:03:43:07 00:03:45:01 - What's your name? - Lawrence.
0023 00:02:31:16 00:02:33:03 OK, come here.	0038 00:03:45:03 00:03:47:23 Lawrence, you ever played keyboards? Any techno?
0024 00:02:35:16 00:02:39:15 - Ever played the electric guitar? - My dad thinks it's a waste of time.	0039 00:03:48:06 00:03:49:18 No, I only play piano.
0025 00:02:39:24 00:02:40:20 A waste of...	0040 00:03:49:20 00:03:53:00 OK. All right, fair enough. Try this out for me, OK?
0026 00:02:42:17 00:02:43:15 Try this one.	0041 00:03:53:09 00:03:56:23 Just give this a try on my count. One, two, three, four.
0027 00:02:45:24 00:02:51:01 OK, here's a guitar pick. You pluck along with me, if you can.	0042 00:03:57:16 00:03:59:03 Yeah.
0028 00:02:52:06 00:02:57:23 ["IRON MAN" BY BLACK SABBATH]	0043 00:03:59:13 00:04:00:21 Yes!
0029 00:03:04:24 00:03:09:10 ["SMOKE ON THE WATER" BY DEEP PURPLE]	0044 00:04:02:14 00:04:04:11 ♪ Tuc-tac-pa-tec-pa-te.
0030 00:03:09:12 00:03:11:02 [GRUNTS]	0045 00:04:04:15 00:04:08:13 ♪ Come on, come on, come on, come on. Now touch me, babe. Fa-ra-fa-ra.
0031 00:03:18:10 00:03:19:22 Yes!	0046 00:04:08:15 00:04:12:23 ♪ Can't you see that I am not afraid? Sha-ka-ka-ka.
0032 00:03:22:10 00:03:28:03 ["HIGHWAY TO HELL" BY AC/DC]	0047 00:04:13:00 00:04:16:09 ♪ Lawrence is good at piano.
0033 00:03:31:15 00:03:33:02 Ah!	

0048 00:04:16:11 00:04:19:08
♪ He shall be rocking in my show.
Ra-ka-ka-ka. ♪

0049 00:04:19:10 00:04:22:23
Stop. That's perfect. You're perfect.
Stay right there, OK?

0050 00:04:23:11 00:04:25:11
You. Could you come up here, please?

0051 00:04:26:08 00:04:28:00
- What was your name?
- Katie.

0052 00:04:28:02 00:04:30:15
Katie, what were you playing,
the big thing?

0053 00:04:30:21 00:04:33:05
- Cello.
- OK. This is a bass guitar.

0054 00:04:33:07 00:04:36:10
It's exactly the same.
But instead of playing like this,

0055 00:04:36:12 00:04:39:12
you tip it on the side,
c-hello-o-o, you've got a bass.

0056 00:04:39:14 00:04:41:01
Try it on.

0057 00:04:42:00 00:04:44:24
OK, now play this note right here.
That's a G.

0058 00:04:45:22 00:04:48:07
OK, but let your fingers
do the rocking.

0059 00:04:48:09 00:04:53:00
Keep that G coming all day long.
G, G, G, G, G, G. Good. Stop.

0060 00:04:53:04 00:04:55:04
Are there any drummers in the house?

0061 00:04:56:04 00:04:57:16
I play percussion.

0062 00:04:57:18 00:05:00:03
- He couldn't play anything else.
- Shut up!

0063 00:05:00:05 00:05:01:17
Come here, dude.

0064 00:05:05:08 00:05:08:08
Just see if you can do what I do.
OK? Just give it a try.

0065 00:05:11:18 00:05:13:09
OK? Give that a try.

0066 00:05:19:13 00:05:22:24
OK! That's really good.
Just stay right here.

0067 00:05:24:10 00:05:27:22
All right, OK.
Lawrence, give me a G note.

0068 00:05:29:06 00:05:30:21
With the fifth above it.

0069 00:05:31:07 00:05:32:19
And the middle one.

0070 00:05:33:04 00:05:36:06
No middle one, I changed my mind.
Now go an octave below.

0071 00:05:36:08 00:05:38:16
Now give me some rhythm.
Pam-pam-pam...

0072 00:05:38:18 00:05:40:10
And keep that same rhythm. Go.

0073 00:05:40:12 00:05:43:11
OK. Katie, remember that note
I taught you, the G?

0074 00:05:43:14 00:05:47:00
Play it, but also keep it rocking.
Good. Pam-pam-pam-pa.

0075 00:05:47:02 00:05:52:09
OK, give me like a...
chung-chik-chung-chik-chung.

0076 00:05:52:12 00:05:55:07 Good. No, bad. That's like George Of The Jungle.	0080 00:06:04:02 00:06:06:08 ["SMOKE ON THE WATER" BY DEEP PURPLE]
0077 00:05:55:09 00:05:57:24 Play it up here on the cymbal, but really light!	0081 00:06:06:08 00:06:11:03 Yes! Yes! Oh... All right, let's go!
0078 00:05:58:11 00:06:00:14 Oh, that's it! OK, keep going with that.	0082 00:06:15:21 00:06:19:10 Oh! All right, stop. Stop!
0079 00:06:00:16 00:06:04:00 Zack, you remember this thing I taught you a minute ago?	

References

Action on Hearing Loss. 2018. 'Access to TV and video on demand (VOD) for people with hearing loss'. https://actiononhearingloss.org.uk/wp-content/uploads/2020/05/TV-and-VOD-Policy-Statement-2018_FINAL.pdf. Accessed 5 August 2020.

Action on Hearing Loss. n.d. 'Facts and figures'. https://www.actiononhearingloss.org.uk/about-us/our-research-and-evidence/facts-and-figures/. Accessed 5 August 2020.

Baker, Robert G., Guy Rowston and Andrew D. Lambourne. 1984. *Handbook for Television Subtitlers*. Winchester: Engineering Division, Independent Broadcasting Authority.

BBC. 2009. 'Online subtitling editorial guidelines'. Version 1.1. https://nanopdf.com/download/bbccouk-online-subtitling-editorial-guidelines-v11_pdf. Accessed 7 October 2020.

BBC. 2010. 'What is the origin and meaning of the pirate expression "shiver me timbers"?' *History Extra*. https://www.historyextra.com/period/victorian/what-is-the-origin-and-meaning-of-the-pirate-expression-shiver-me-timbers. Accessed 24 August 2020.

BBC. 2011. 'Cinema subtitle glasses give promise to deaf film fans'. BBC News, 25 August. https://www.bbc.com/news/av/technology-14654339/cinema-subtitle-glasses-give-promise-to-deaf-film-fans. Accessed 5 August 2020.

BBC. 2019. 'Subtitle guidelines'. Version 1.1.8. https://bbc.github.io/subtitle-guidelines/. Accessed 5 August 2020.

BBC. 2020. 'Commissioning for 6–16 year-olds'. https://www.bbc.co.uk/commissioning/tv/articles/cbbc. Accessed 23 August 2020.

BCIG. 2018. 'BCIG annual data collection: Financial year 2017–2018'. British Cochlear Implant Group. https://www.bcig.org.uk/wp-content/uploads/2019/02/2018.09.18-Report-to-Council-Data-Collection-FY17-18a.pdf. Accessed 7 October 2020.

BDA. 2018. 'BDA response to Independent article – 12/03/2018'. British Deaf Association. https://bda.org.uk/bda-response-independent-article-12-03-2018. Accessed 22 August 2020.

BDA. 2020. 'Help & resources for sign language'. British Deaf Association. https://bda.org.uk/help-resources/. Accessed 5 August 2020.

Bélanger, Nathalie N. and Keith Rayner. 2015. 'What eye movements reveal about deaf readers'. *Current Directions in Psychological Science* 24 (3): 220–6. https://journals.sagepub.com/doi/10.1177/0963721414567527. Accessed 7 October 2020.

Boatner, Edmund B. 1950. 'Captioned films for the deaf'. *American Annals of the Deaf* 96 (3): 346–52. https://dcmp.org/learn/253-captioned-films-for-the-deaf. Accessed 5 August 2020.

Brennan, Mary. 2003. 'Deafness, disability and inclusion: the gap between rhetoric and practice'. *Policy Futures in Education* 1 (4): 668–85. https://doi.org/10.2304/pfie.2003.1.4.5.

Brown, Will. 2017. 'What does title-safe mean for subtitles & on-screen title translation?' JBI Studios' Blog. 8 June. https://jbilocalization.com/blog/what-does-title-safe-mean-for-subtitles-on-screen-title-translation/. Accessed 5 August 2020.

Canadian Association of the Deaf. 2015. 'Cochlear implants'. http://cad.ca/issues-positions/cochlear-implants. Accessed 5 August 2020.

Channel 4. n.d. 'Channel 4 subtitling guidelines for foreign-language programmes'. https://www.channel4.com/media/documents/corporate/foi-docs/SG_FLP.pdf. Accessed 5 August 2020.

Clark, Joe. 2006. 'What's wrong with Tiresias?' Screenfont.Ca. http://screenfont.ca/fonts/today/Tiresias. Accessed 5 August 2020.

Commonwealth Government of Australia. 1992. 'Disability Discrimination Act 1992'. http://www8.austlii.edu.au/cgi-bin/viewdb/au/legis/cth/consol_act/dda1992264.

CRIDE. 2015. 'CRIDE report on 2015 survey on educational provision for deaf children: 2015 UK-wide summary'. Consortium for Research into Deaf Education. https://www.ndcs.org.uk/media/1851/cride_2015_uk_wide_summary.pdf. Accessed 5 August 2020.

CRIDE. 2017. 'CRIDE report on 2017 survey on educational provision for deaf children: 2017 UK-wide summary'. Consortium for Research into Deaf Education. https://www.ndcs.org.uk/media/4151/cride-2017-uk-report-final.pdf. Accessed 5 August 2020.

CRTC. 2007. 'Broadcasting public notice CRTC 2007-54'. Canadian Radio-television and Telecommunications Commission. https://crtc.gc.ca/eng/archive/2007/pb2007-54.htm. Accessed 5 August 2020.

CRTC. 2015. 'Broadcasting regulatory policy CRTC 2015-104'. Canadian Radio-television and Telecommunications Commission. https://crtc.gc.ca/eng/archive/2015/2015-104.htm. Accessed 5 August 2020.

CSA. 2018. 'Le sous-titrage'. Conseil Supérieur de l'Audiovisuel. 2018. https://www.csa.fr/Proteger/Garantie-des-droits-et-libertes/Les-droits-des-personnes-handicapees/Le-sous-titrage. Accessed 5 August 2020.

Delabastita, Dirk. 1989. 'Translation and mass-communication: film and T.V. translation as evidence of cultural dynamics'. *Babel* 35 (4): 193–218. https://benjamins.com/catalog/babel.35.4.02del. Accessed 7 October 2020.

De Linde, Zoé and Neil Kay. 1999. *The Semiotics of Subtitling*. Manchester: St Jerome.

Department of Justice, Civil Rights Division. 2016. 'Nondiscrimination on the basis of disability by public accommodations: Movie theaters; movie captioning and audio description'. https://www.ada.gov/regs2016/movie_rule.htm. Accessed 5 August 2020.

Díaz Cintas, Jorge, Pilar Orero and Aline Remael, eds. 2007. *Media for All: Subtitling for the deaf, audio description, and sign language*. Approaches to Translation Studies 30. Amsterdam: Rodopi.

Díaz-Cintas, Jorge and Aline Remael. 2007. *Audiovisual Translation: Subtitling*. Translation Practices Explained 11. Manchester: St Jerome.

Díaz Cintas, Jorge and Aline Remael. 2014. *Audiovisual Translation: Subtitling*. London: Routledge.

Disabled World. 2016. 'Cinema subtitle system for the hard of hearing'. *Disabled World*, 1st April. https://www.disabled-world.com/disability/investors/cinema-subtitles.php. Accessed 5 August 2020.

Dolnick, Edward. 1993. 'Deafness as culture'. *Atlantic Monthly*, September: 37–53. http://courses.washington.edu/intro2ds/Readings/Deafness_as_culture.pdf. Accessed 5 August 2020.

Downey, Gregory John. 2008. *Closed Captioning: Subtitling, stenography, and the digital convergence of text with television*. Johns Hopkins Studies in the History of Technology. Baltimore: Johns Hopkins University Press.

DPP. 2020. Delivery requirements. File based programme delivery using AMWA AS-11. Version 6.0.1. Digital Production Partnership. https://www.thedpp.com/filedelivery/fd-uk. Accessed 7 October 2020.

d'Ydewalle, Géry and Marijke Van de Poel. 1999. 'Incidental foreign-language acquisition by children watching subtitled television programs'. *Journal of Psycholinguistic Research* 28 (3): 227–44. https://psycnet.apa.org/doi/10.1023/A:1023202130625. Accessed 7 October 2020.

EFHOH. 2015. 'State of subtitling access in EU: 2015 report'. European Federation of Hard of Hearing People. https://efhoh.org/wp-content/uploads/2017/01/EFHOH-State-of-Subtitling-2015-English.pdf. Accessed 5 August 2020.

Encyclopædia Britannica. 2015. 'Intonation'. Encyclopædia Britannica. 25 August. https://www.britannica.com/topic/intonation. Accessed 5 August 2020.

EUD. 2013. 'Cochlear implant'. European Union of the Deaf. May. https://www.eud.eu/about-us/eud-position-paper/cochlear-implant-position-paper. Accessed 5 August 2020.

EURO CIU. 2017. 'What is the cochlear implant?' European Association of Cochlear Implant Users. http://eurociu.eu/what-is-the-ci-. Accessed 5 August 2020.

European Commission. 2016. 'Proposal for a directive of the European Parliament and of the Council amending Directive 2010/13/EU on the coordination of certain provisions laid down by law, regulation or administrative action in Member States concerning the provision of audiovisual media services in view of changing market realities.' 2016/0151 (COD). https://eur-lex.europa.eu/legal-content/EN/TXT/PDF/?uri=CELEX:52016PC0287&from=EN. Accessed 5 August 2020.

European Union. 2009. 'Commission recommendation of 28 October 2009 facilitating the release of the digital dividend in the European Union'. *Official Journal of the European Union*, 24 November. https://eur-lex.europa.eu/LexUriServ/LexUriServ.do?uri=OJ:L:2009:308:0024:0026:EN:PDF. Accessed 20 August 2020.

European Union. 2010. 'Directive 2010/13/EU of the European Parliament and of the Council of 10 March 2010 on the coordination of certain provisions laid down by law, regulation or administrative action in Member States concerning the provision of audiovisual media services.' *Official Journal of the European Union*, 15 April. https://eur-lex.europa.eu/legal-content/EN/TXT/PDF/?uri=CELEX:32010L0013&from=EN. Accessed 5 August 2020.

European Union. 2018. 'Directive (EU) 2018/1808 of the European Parliament and of the Council of 14 November 2018 amending Directive 2010/13/EU on the coordination of certain provisions laid down by law, regulation or administrative action in Member States concerning the provision of audiovisual media services (Audiovisual Media Services Directive) in view of changing market realities'. PE/33/2018/REV/1' *Official Journal of the European Union*, 28 November. http://data.europa.eu/eli/dir/2018/1808/oj. Accessed 5 August 2020.

European Union. 2019. 'Directive 2019/882 of the European Parliament and of the Council of 17 April 2019 on the accessibility requirements for products and services.' *Official Journal of the European Union*, 7 June. https://www.europarl.europa.eu/RegData/etudes/BRIE/2017/603973/EPRS_BRI(2017)603973_EN.pdf. Accessed 28 August 2020.

Finkelstein, Victor. 1980. *Attitudes and Disabled People: Issues for discussion*. New York: World Rehabilitation Fund.

Gottlieb, Henrik. 1994. 'Subtitling: Diagonal translation'. *Perspectives: Studies in Translatology* 2 (1): 101–21.

Gottlieb, Henrik. 1997. *Subtitles, Translation & Idioms*. Copenhagen: Center for Translation Studies and Lexicography, Department of English, University of Copenhagen.

GPO. 2019. 'Electronic Code of Federal Regulations'. Government Publishing Office. https://www.ecfr.gov/cgi-bin/ECFR. Accessed 5 August 2020.

Hearing Link. 2018. 'Facts about deafness & hearing loss'. https://www.hearinglink.org/your-hearing/about-hearing/facts-about-deafness-hearing-loss. Accessed 5 August 2020.

Holland, Maureen. 2015. 'Concerts for the deaf: introducing the Emoti-Chair'. CMUSE, 25 November. https://www.cmuse.org/concerts-for-the-deaf-introducing-the-emoti-chair. Accessed 5 August 2020.

Huckvale, Mark. 2017. 'HearLoss – hearing loss demonstrator'. UCL Psychology and Language Sciences. 12 April 2017. https://www.phon.ucl.ac.uk/resource/hearloss. Accessed 5 August 2020.

ITU. 2020. 'Status of the transition to digital terrestrial television (DSO)'. International Telecommunication Union. https://www.itu.int/en/ITU-D/Spectrum-Broadcasting/DSO/Pages/dataminer.aspx. Accessed 7 October 2020.

Ivarsson, Jan. 2004. 'A short technical history of subtitles in Europe'. TransEdit. https://www.scribd.com/document/421309119/A-Short-Technical-History-of-Subtitling-in-Europe. Accessed 10 September 2020.

Ivarsson, Jan and Mary Carroll. 1998. *Subtitling*. Simrishamn: TransEdit.

Jakobson, Roman. 1959. 'On linguistic aspects of translation'. In Reuben A. Brower (ed.), *On Translation*, 232–9. Harvard Studies in Comparative Literature 23. Cambridge, MA: Harvard University Press.

JTC. 2012. 'Audiogram of familiar sounds'. John Tracy Clinic, Los Angeles. https://www.jtc.org/wp-content/uploads/2015/11/Audiogram_What_Does_Child_Hear.pdf. Accessed 5 August 2020.

Karamitroglou, Fotios. 1998. 'A proposed set of subtitling standards in Europe'. *Translation Journal* 2 (2). http://translationjournal.net/journal/04stndrd.htm. Accessed 7 October 2020.

Koolstra, Cees M. and Johannes W. J. Beentjes. 1999. 'Children's vocabulary acquisition in a foreign language through watching subtitled television programs at home'. *Educational Technology Research and Development* 47 (1): 51–60. https://doi.org/10.1007/BF02299476. Accessed 7 October 2020.

Koolstra, Cees M., Tom H. A. van der Voort and Leo J. Th. van der Kamp. 1997. 'Television's impact on children's reading comprehension and decoding skills: a 3-year panel study'. *Reading Research Quarterly* 32 (2): 128–52. https://doi.org/10.1598/RRQ.32.2.1. Accessed 7 October 2020.

Kovačič, Irena. 1994. 'Relevance as a factor in subtitling reductions'. In *Teaching Translation and Interpreting 2: Insights, aims, visions*, edited by Cay Dollerup and Annette Lindegaard, 245–52. Amsterdam: John Benjamins.

Kovalik, Gail L. 1992. '"Silent" films revisited: captioned films for the deaf'. *Library Trends* 41 (1): 110–17. https://dcmp.org/learn/211-silent-films-revisited-captioned-films-for-the-deaf. Accessed 7 October 2020.

Krejtz, Izabela, Agnieszka Szarkowska and Krzysztof Krejtz. 2013. 'The effects of shot changes on eye movements in subtitling'. *Journal of Eye Movement Research* 6 (5): 1–12. https://doi.org/10.16910/jemr.6.5.3. Accessed 7 October 2020.

Kuo, Arista Szu-Yu. 2017. 'Subtitling quality beyond the linguistic dimension'. In *The Routledge Handbook of Chinese Translation*, ed. Chris Shei and Zhao-Ming Gao, 415–31. Abingdon: Routledge. http://hdl.handle.net/10220/49955. Accessed 7 October 2020.

Marsh, Alison. 2006. 'Respeaking for the BBC'. *InTRAlinea*, special issue: Respeaking, ed. Carlo Eugeni and Gabriele Mack. http://www.intralinea.org/specials/article/1700. Accessed 5 August 2020.

McCormack, Abby and Heather Fortnum. 2013. 'Why do people fitted with hearing aids not wear them?' *International Journal of Audiology* 52 (5): 360–8. https://doi.org/10.3109/14992027 .2013.769066. Accessed 7 October 2020.

Moniteur Belge. 2007. 'Loi tendant à lutter contre certaines formes de discrimination'. http:// www.ejustice.just.fgov.be/cgi_loi/change_lg.pl?language=fr&la=F&cn=2007051035& table_name=loi#:~:text=3.La%20pr%C3%A9sente%20loi%20a,la%20conviction%20 syndicale%2C%5D1%20la. Accessed 7 October 2020.

NDCS. 2016. 'Right from the start: A campaign to improve early years support for deaf children'. National Deaf Children's Society. https://www.ndcs.org.uk/media/1283/right_from_the_ start_campaign_report_final.pdf. Accessed 22 August 2020.

NDCS. 2019. 'Cochlear implants'. National Deaf Children's Society. http://www.ndcs.org.uk/ information-and-support/childhood-deafness/hearing-implants/cochlear-implants. Accessed 11 August 2020.

Netflix. 2020a. 'English timed text style guide'. https://partnerhelp.netflixstudios.com/hc/en-us/ articles/217350977-English-Timed-Text-Style-Guide. Accessed 11 August 2020.

Netflix. 2020b. 'Timed text style guide: general requirements'. https://partnerhelp.netflixstudios. com/hc/en-us/articles/215758617-Timed-Text-Style-Guide-General-Requirements. Accessed 11 August 2020.

Neuman, Susan B. and Patricia Koskinen. 1992. 'Captioned television as comprehensible input: effects of incidental word learning from context for language minority students'. *Reading Research Quarterly* 27 (1): 95–106. https://www.jstor.org/stable/747835. Accessed 7 October 2020.

Neves, Josélia. 2008. '10 fallacies about subtitling for the d/Deaf and the hard of hearing'. *Journal of Specialised Translation* 10: 128–43. https://www.jostrans.org/issue10/art_neves.pdf. Accessed 7 October 2020.

NHS. 2018. 'Newborn hearing screening'. 23 February. https://www.nhs.uk/conditions/ pregnancy-and-baby/newborn-hearing-test. Accessed 11 August 2020.

Ofcom. 2017. 'Ofcom's code on television access services'. Office of Communications. https:// www.ofcom.org.uk/__data/assets/pdf_file/0020/97040/Access-service-code-Jan-2017.pdf. Accessed 11 August 2020.

Ofcom. 2018. 'Statement: making on-demand services accessible'. 20 December. Office of Communications. https://www.ofcom.org.uk/consultations-and-statements/category-1/odps- accessibility. Accessed 11 August 2020.

Oliver, Michael. 1990. *The Politics of Disablement*. Basingstoke: Macmillan. https://doi.org/ 10.1007/978-1-349-20895-1. Accessed 7 October 2020.

Oliver, Mike. 2013. 'The social model of disability: thirty years on'. *Disability & Society* 28 (7): 1024–6. https://doi.org/10.1080/09687599.2013.818773. Accessed 7 October 2020.

ONS. 2018. 'Overview of the UK population: November 2018'. Office for National Statistics. hhttps://www.ons.gov.uk/releases/overviewoftheukpopulationnovember2018. Accessed 7 October 2020.

Oxford University Press, Academic Division. 2014. 'Guide for authors and editors: Oxford Paperback Reference'. Oxford University Press. https://www.oxfordreference.com/fileasset/ files/QuickReference_AuthorGuidelines.pdf. Accessed 11 August 2020.

Paivio, Allan. 1991. 'Dual coding theory: retrospect and current status'. *Canadian Journal of Psychology/Revue Canadienne de Psychologie* 45 (3): 255–87. https://doi.org/10.1037/ h0084295. Accessed 7 October 2020.

Paivio, Allan. 2014. *Mind and Its Evolution: A dual coding theoretical approach*. New York/Hove: Psychology Press.

Paivio, Allan and Wallace Lambert. 1981. 'Dual coding and bilingual memory'. *Journal of Verbal Learning and Verbal Behavior* 20 (5): 532–9. https://doi.org/10.1016/S0022-5371(81) 90156-0. Accessed 7 October 2020.

Poyatos, Fernando. 1993. *Paralanguage: A linguistic and interdisciplinary approach to interactive speech and sound*. Current Issues in Linguistic Theory 92. Amsterdam: John Benjamins.

Poyatos, Fernando. 2008. *Textual Translation and Live Translation: The total experience of nonverbal communication in literature, theater and cinema*. Amsterdam: John Benjamins.

Raad van State [Council of State]. 2008. 'Mediabesluit 2008' [media decision 2008]. Algemene maatregel van bestuur (AMvB) [order in council]. https://wetten.overheid.nl/BWBR0025036/2014-01-01. Accessed 11 August 2020.

Raine, Chris. 2013. 'Cochlear implants in the United Kingdom: Awareness and utilization'. *Cochlear Implants International* 14 (sup1): S32–S37. https://doi.org/10.1179/1467010013Z.00000000077. Accessed 7 October 2020.

Remael, Aline. 2007. 'Sampling subtitling for the deaf and the hard-of-hearing in Europe'. In *Media for All: Subtitling for the deaf, audio description, and sign language*, edited by Jorge Díaz Cintas, Pilar Orero and Aline Remael, 23–52. Amsterdam: Rodopi.

Robert, Isabelle S., Iris Schrijver and Ella Diels. 2019. 'Live subtitlers: who are they? A survey study'. *Linguistica Antverpiensia, New Series – Themes in Translation Studies* 18. https://lans-tts.uantwerpen.be/index.php/LANS-TTS/article/view/544. Accessed 7 October 2020.

Roberts, Adrian. 2008. 'Synopsis of causation: sensorineural hearing loss'. Ministry of Defence. https://assets.publishing.service.gov.uk/government/uploads/system/uploads/attachment_data/file/384550/sensorineural_hearing_loss.pdf. Accessed 5 August 2020.

Romero-Fresco, Pablo. 2011. *Subtitling through Speech Recognition: Respeaking*. St Jerome.

Romero-Fresco. 2012. 'Respeaking in translator training curricula: present and future prospects'. *Interpreter and Translator Trainer* 6 (1): 91–112. https://doi.org/10.1080/13556509.2012.10798831. Accessed 7 October 2020.

Romero-Fresco. 2013. 'Accessible filmmaking: joining the dots between audiovisual translation, accessibility and filmmaking'. *Journal of Specialised Translations* 20 (July): 201–23. https://www.jostrans.org/issue20/art_romero.pdf. Accessed 7 October 2020.

Romero-Fresco. 2018. 'Respeaking: Subtitling through speech recognition'. In *The Routledge Handbook of Audiovisual Translation*, edited by Luis Pérez-González, 96–113. Abingdon: Routledge.

Romero-Fresco, Pablo, Sabela Melchor-Couto, Hayley Dawson, Zoe Moores and Inma Pedregosa. 2019. 'Respeaking certification: bringing together training, research and practice'. *Linguistica Antverpiensia, New Series – Themes in Translation Studies* 18: 216–36. https://lans-tts.uantwerpen.be/index.php/LANS-TTS/article/view/514. Accessed 7 October 2020.

Sandford, James. 2015. 'The impact of subtitle display rate on enjoyment under normal television viewing conditions'. BBC Research & Development White Paper WHP 306. https://www.bbc.co.uk/rd/publications/whitepaper306. Accessed 5 August 2020.

Shannan, Brian. 2010. 'Audiology – a curriculum for excellence'. Scottish Sensory Centre. http://www.ssc.education.ed.ac.uk/courses/deaf/dnov10i.html. Accessed 5 August 2020.

Silver, Janet, John Gill, Christopher Sharville, James Slater and Michael Martin. 1998. 'A new font for digital television subtitles'. Unpublished paper.

Stagetext. n.d. 'History of Stagetext'. http://www.stagetext.org/about-stagetext/history-of-stagetext. Accessed 12 August 2020.

Stagetext. 2015. 'Stagetext: CaptionCue: research and development report'. https://drive.google.com/file/d/0B4LaBZqbWFnDSW9Wb3pNdmZwc2c/view?pli=1. Accessed 7 October 2020.

Stagetext. 2019a. 'Peter Pullan writes about the Puppet Theatre Barge'. http://www.stagetext.org/news/456-peter-pullan-writes-about-the-puppet-theatre-barge. Accessed 5 August 2020.

Stagetext. 2019b. 'The role of the captioner'. http://www.stagetext.org/the-role-of-the-captioner. Accessed 5 August 2020.

Swedish Press and Broadcasting Authority. 2016. 'Requirements regarding accessibility of television broadcasts for persons with functional impairments: Decision', 29 June. https://www.mprt.se/documents/tillg%C3%A4nglighet/16%2001344%20tillg%C3%A4nglighetsbeslutet_english.pdf?epslanguage=sv. Accessed 28 August 2020.

Szarkowska, Agnieszka. 2013. 'Towards interlingual subtitling for the deaf and the hard of hearing'. *Perspectives* 21 (1): 68–81. https://doi.org/10.1080/0907676X.2012.722650. Accessed 7 October 2020.

Szarkowska, Agnieszka and Olivia Gerber-Morón. 2018. 'Viewers can keep up with fast subtitles: evidence from eye movements'. *PloS One* 13 (6): e0199331. https://doi.org/10.1371/journal.pone.0199331. Accessed 5 August 2020.

Talking Birds. n.d. 'The Difference Engine'. Talking Birds. https://differenceengineaccess.wordpress.com. Accessed 5 August 2020.

TDF. 2020. 'Open caption information sheet: information, statistics, pricing'. https://www.tdf.org/nyc/95/open-caption-information-sheet. Accessed 5 August 2020.

Teatro Accesible. 2020. 'Quiénes somos.' http://www.teatroaccesible.com/es/about/whoweare. Accessed 7 October 2020.

Tidy, Colin. 2014. 'Deafness in children'. Patient, 21 March. https://patient.info/doctor/deafness-in-children. Accessed 7 October 2020.

UK Parliament. 1990. 'Broadcasting Act 1990'. http://www.legislation.gov.uk/ukpga/1990/42/contents. Accessed 6 August 2020.

UK Parliament. 1995. 'Disability Discrimination Act 1995'. https://www.legislation.gov.uk/ukpga/1995/50/contents. Accessed 7 October 2020.

UK Parliament. 2003. 'Communications Act 2003'. http://www.legislation.gov.uk/ukpga/2003/21/section/303. Accessed 6 August 2020.

UK Parliament. 2010. 'Equality Act 2010'. http://www.legislation.gov.uk/ukpga/2010/15/contents. Accessed 6 August 2020.

UK Parliament. 2017. 'Digital Economy Act 2017'. http://www.legislation.gov.uk/ukpga/2017/30/pdfs/ukpga_20170030_en.pdf. Accessed 6 August 2020.

UKCA. 2018. 'UK Cinema Association launches subtitling challenge fund'. UK Cinema Association, 16 July. https://www.cinemauk.org.uk/2018/07/uk-cinema-association-launches-subtitling-challenge-fund/. Accessed 11 August 2020.

Union of the Physically Impaired Against Segregation. 1974. 'Aims' and 'Policy statement'. https://disability-studies.leeds.ac.uk/wp-content/uploads/sites/40/library/UPIAS-UPIAS.pdf. Accessed 6 August 2020.

United Nations. 2006a. 'Convention on the Rights of Persons with Disabilities – Articles'. https://www.un.org/development/desa/disabilities/convention-on-the-rights-of-persons-with-disabilities/convention-on-the-rights-of-persons-with-disabilities-2.html. Accessed 6 August 2020.

United Nations. 2006b. 'Convention on the Rights of Persons with Disabilities and Optional Protocol'. https://www.un.org/disabilities/documents/convention/convoptprot-e.pdf. Accessed 6 August 2020.

United Nations. 2016. '10th anniversary of the adoption of Convention on the Rights of Persons with Disabilities (CRPD)'. https://www.un.org/development/desa/disabilities/convention-on-the-rights-of-persons-with-disabilities/the-10th-anniversary-of-the-adoption-of-convention-on-the-rights-of-persons-with-disabilities-crpd-crpd-10.html. Accessed 6 August 2020.

United Nations. 2020a. 'Ratifications and signatures of the Convention on the Rights of Persons with Disabilities'. https://treaties.un.org/Pages/ViewDetails.aspx?src=IND&mtdsg_no=IV-15&chapter=4. Accessed 7 October 2020.

United Nations. 2020b. 'Ratifications and signatures of the Optional Protocol to the Convention on the Rights of Persons with Disabilities'. https://treaties.un.org/pages/ViewDetails.aspx?src=TREATY&mtdsg_no=IV-15-a&chapter=4. Accessed 7 October 2020.

United States Congress. 1990. 'Americans with Disabilities Act of 1990, as amended'. https://www.ada.gov/pubs/adastatute08.htm. Accessed 6 August 2020.

VRM (Vlaamse Regulator voor de Media). 2009. 'Decreet betreffende radio-omroep en televisie' [Decree concerning radio broadcasting and television]. https://codex.vlaanderen.be/Portals/Codex/documenten/1017858.html. Accessed 6 August 2020.

VRM. 2012. 'Decreet houdende wijziging van diverse bepalingen van het decreet van 27 maart 2009 betreffende radio-omroep en televisie' [Decree amending various provisions of the Decree of 27 March 2009 concerning radio broadcasting and television]. https://cjsm.be/media/sites/cjsm.media/files/public/mediadecreet_wijziging_20120713.pdf. Accessed 6 August 2020.

W3C. 2016. 'Understanding WCAG 2.0: a guide to understanding and implementing Web Content Accessibility Guidelines 2.0'. https://www.w3.org/TR/UNDERSTANDING-WCAG20/. Accessed 6 August 2020.

Wald, Mike and Keith Bain. 2005. 'Using automatic speech recognition to assist communication and learning'. In HCI International 2005: 11th International Conference on Human–Computer Interaction, Las Vegas, 21–27 July, edited by Gavriel Salvendy. Mahwah, NJ: Lawrence Erlbaum Associates. https://eprints.soton.ac.uk/260730/. Accessed 6 August 2020.

WHO. 2013. 'Millions of people in the world have hearing loss that can be treated or prevented'. World Health Organization. https://www.who.int/pbd/deafness/news/Millionslivewithhearingloss.pdf. Accessed 6 August 2020.

WHO. 2020. 'Deafness and hearing loss'. World Health Organization. 15 March 2018. https://www.who.int/news-room/fact-sheets/detail/deafness-and-hearing-loss. Accessed 28 August 2020.

Films and other audiovisual material

Ai-Media (media company) 2017. *How Deaf People Enjoy Music.* https://www.facebook.com/watch/?v=10155585526449220

Akiyama, Bruce (writer) 2000. 'Nerves of Steal', episode two b, season five. *Arthur.*

BBC (production company). 1958–present. *Blue Peter.*

BBC (production company). 2004–2007. *The Catherine Tate Show.*

BBC TV (production company). 1979. *Quietly in Switzerland.*

Browning, Tod (director). 1931. *Dracula.*

Crosland, Alan (director). 1927. *The Jazz Singer.*

Gold, Elon (comedian). 2014. 'Languages'. *Chosen & Taken.* https://www.youtube.com/watch?v=9oDjrvIqeIs

Hand, David (director). 1942. *Bambi.*

Hazanavicius, Michel (director). 2011. *The Artist.*

Holleyman, Sonia (creator). 2000. 'The Lost Pirates', episode 21 b, season one. *Mona The Vampire.*

Linklater, Richard (director). 2003. *School of Rock.*

Noisey (media company) 2016. *Chris Fonseca – A Short Film About A Deaf Dancer.* https://www.youtube.com/watch?v=lBBpAu9LCN0

Overton, Chris (director). 2017. *The Silent Child.*

Porter, Edwin S. (director). 1903. *Uncle Tom's Cabin.*

Romero-Fresco, Pablo (director). 2012. *Joining the Dots.* https://vimeo.com/64222807. Accessed 6 August 2020.

Scorsese, Martin (director). 1980. *Raging Bull.*

Stagetext (production company). 2015. *The Founding of Stagetext: 'It's like day and night …'.* https://www.youtube.com/watch?v=4dkk5XN4x_0. Accessed 6 August 2020.

TED. 2003. *How to Truly Listen.* By Evelyn Glennie. https://www.ted.com/talks/evelyn_glennie_how_to_truly_listen

WGBH (production company). 1972. *The French Chef.*

Index

Lightning Source UK Ltd.
Milton Keynes UK
UKHW021347150121
377052UK00003B/74